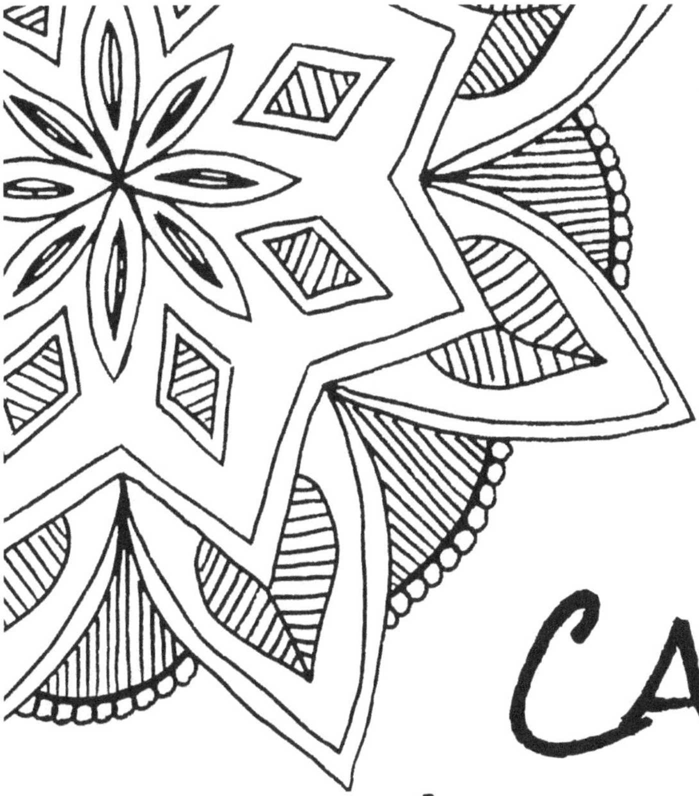

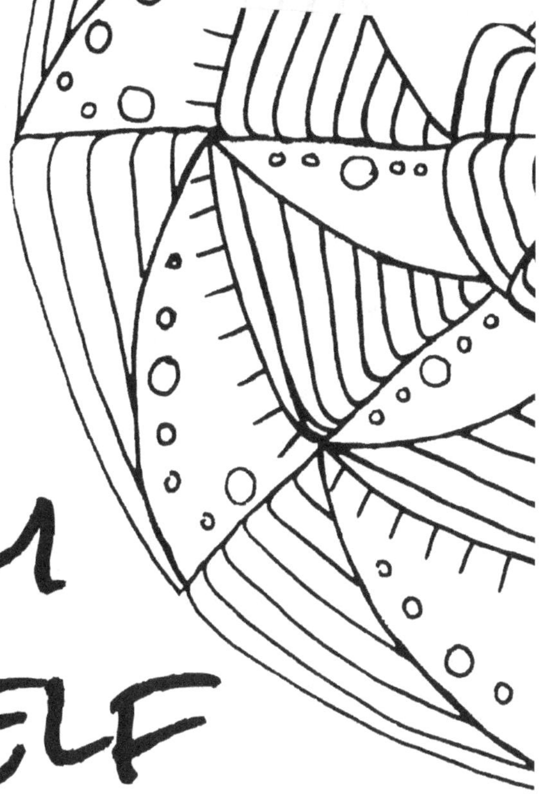

# Calm yourself Colorful

Petra Monaco

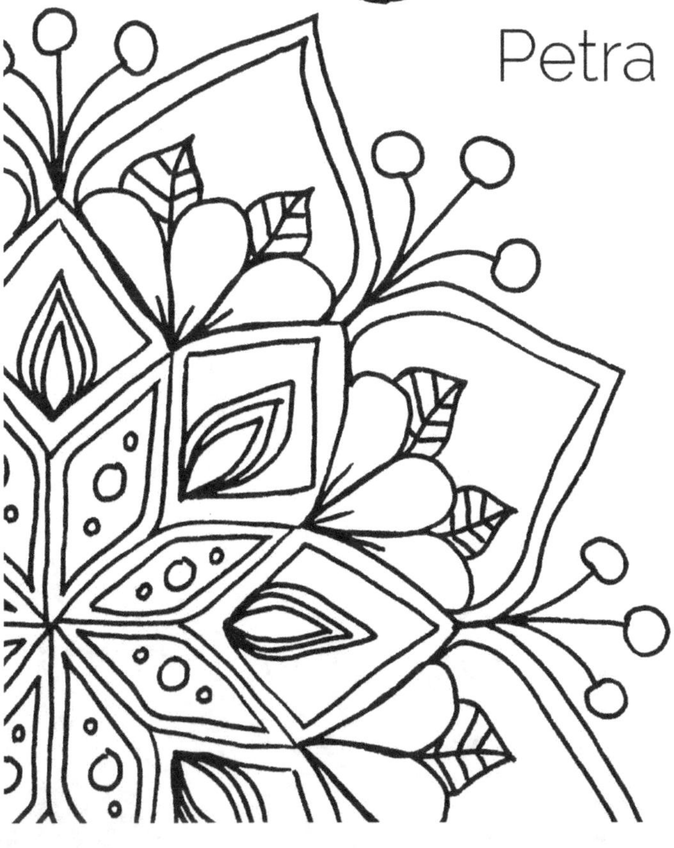

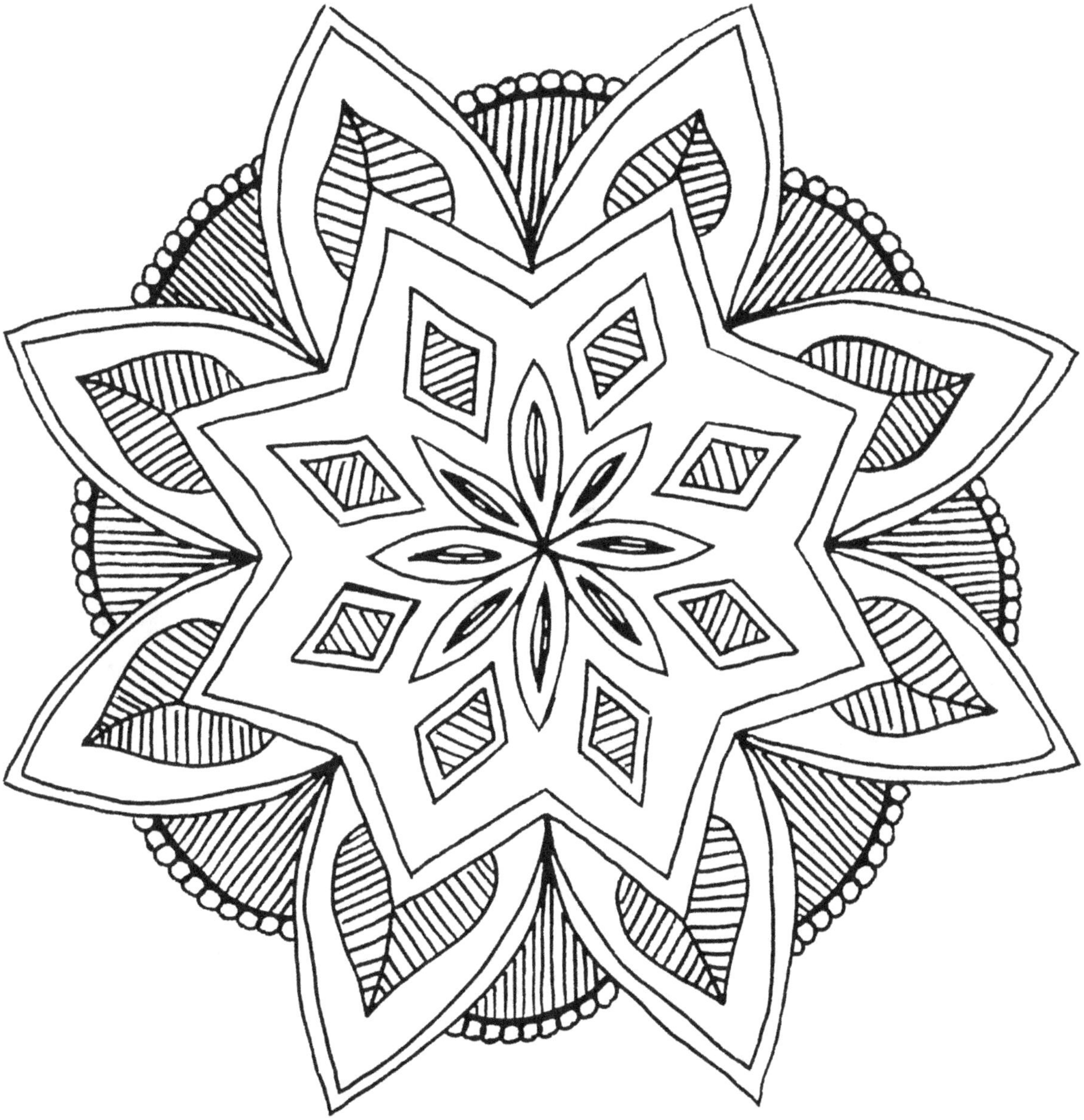

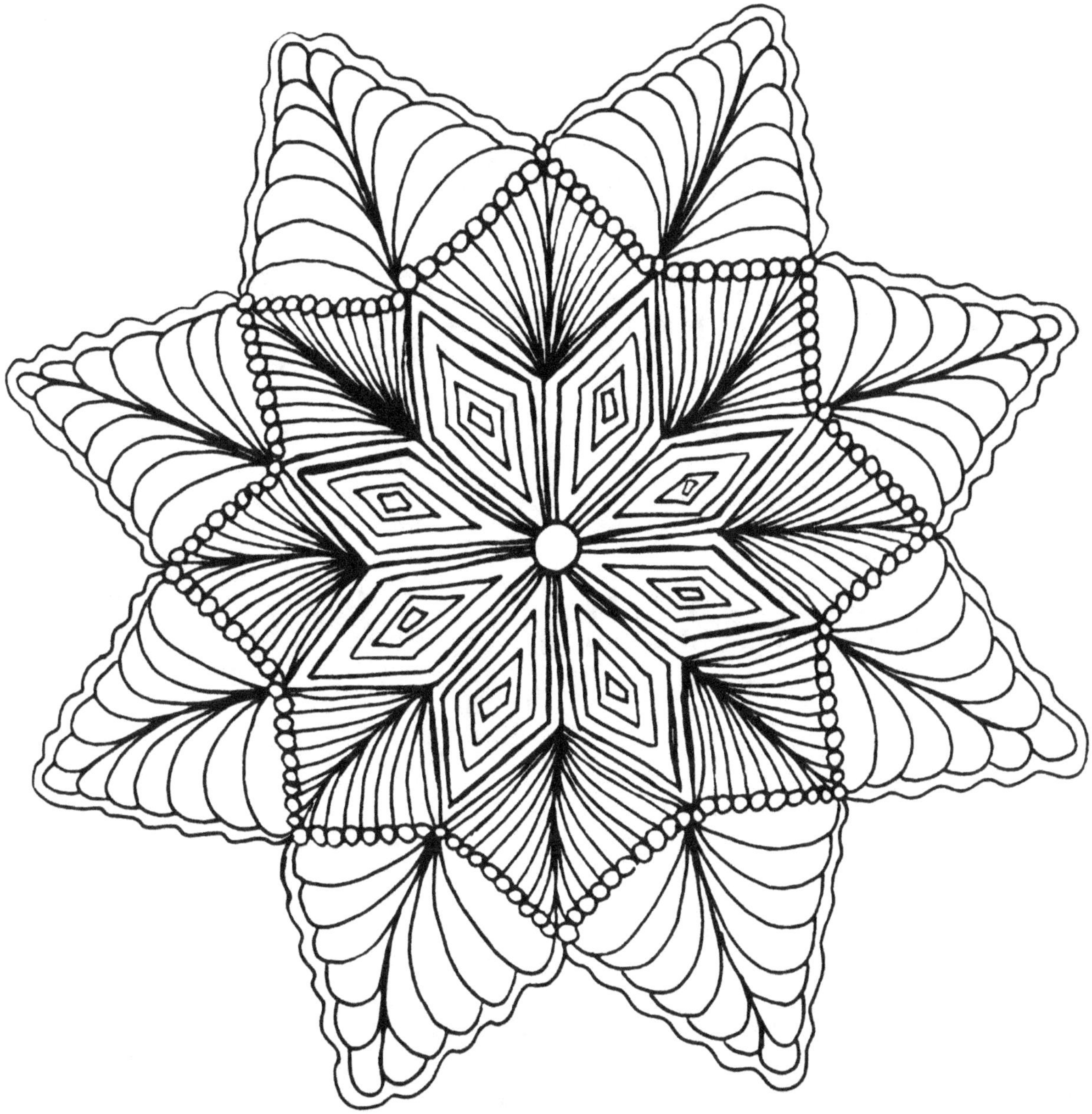

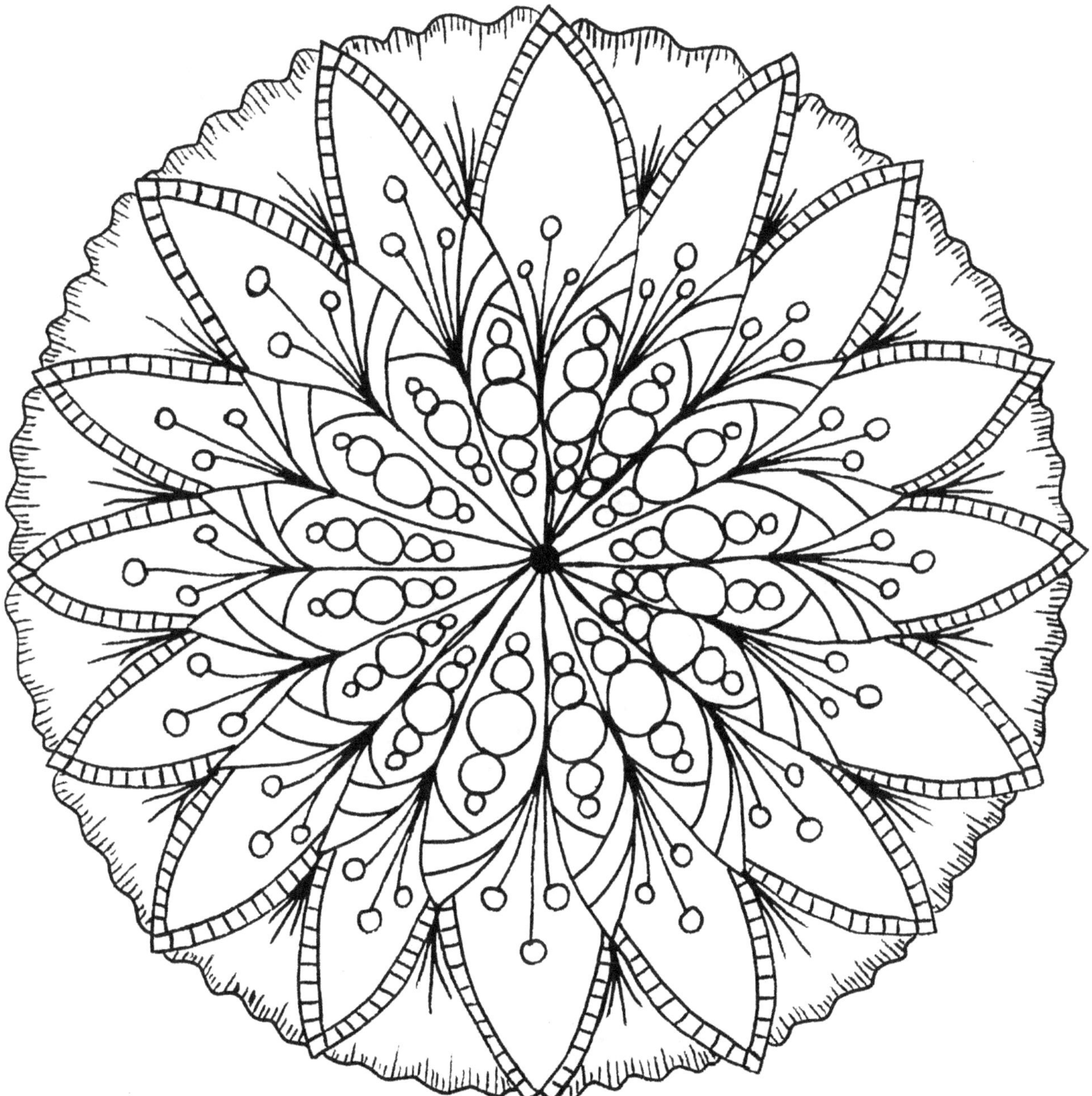

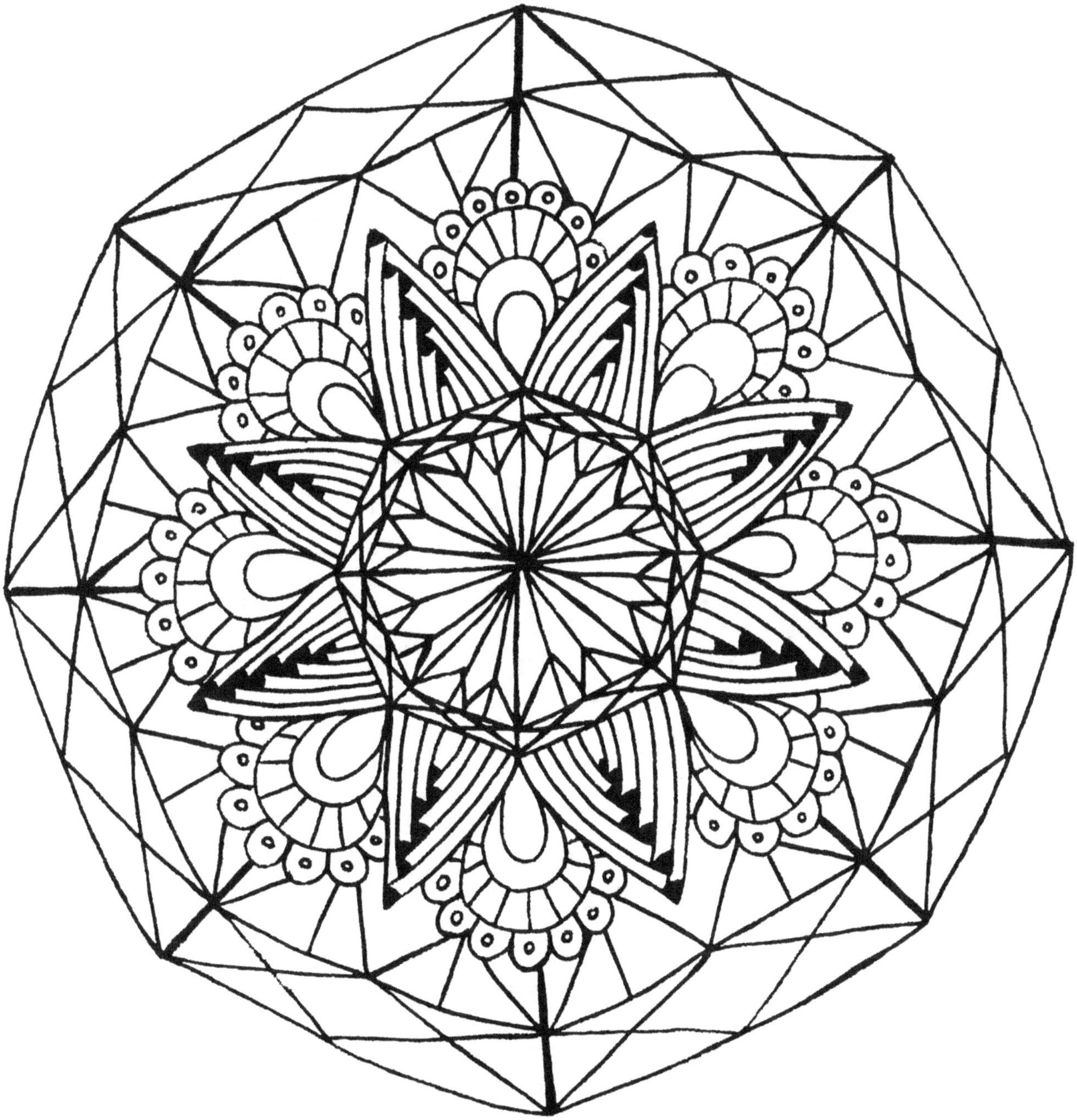

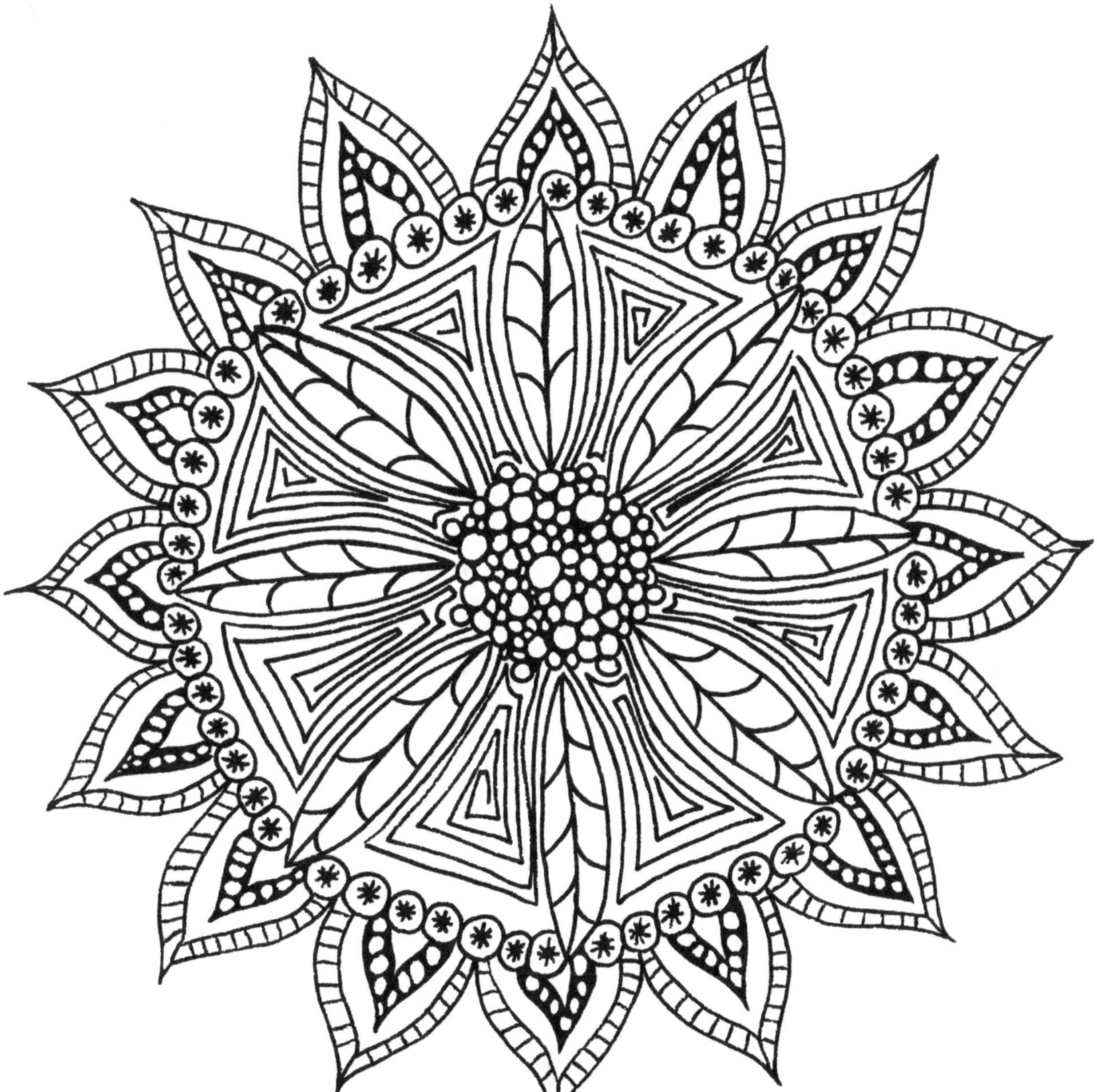

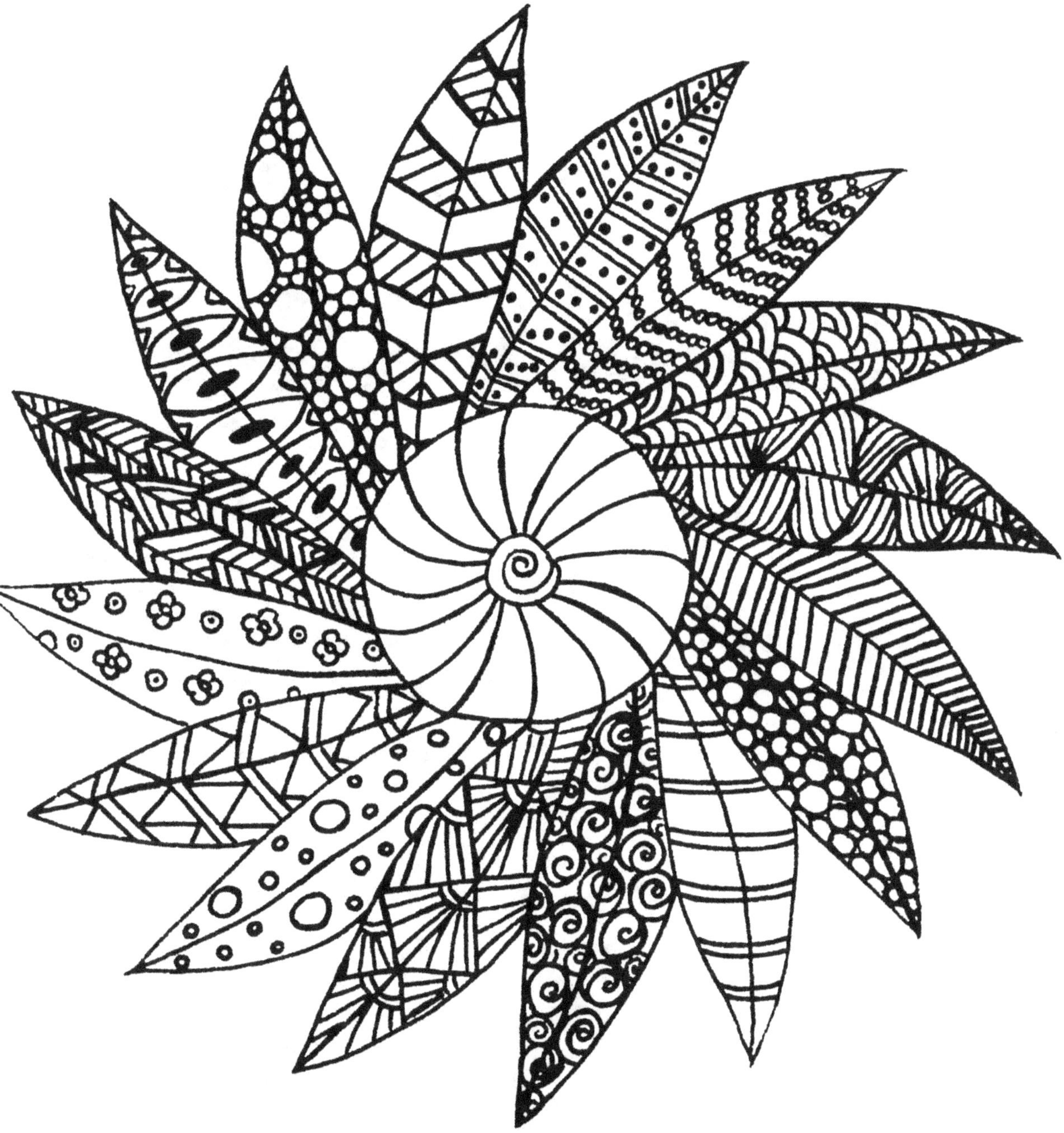

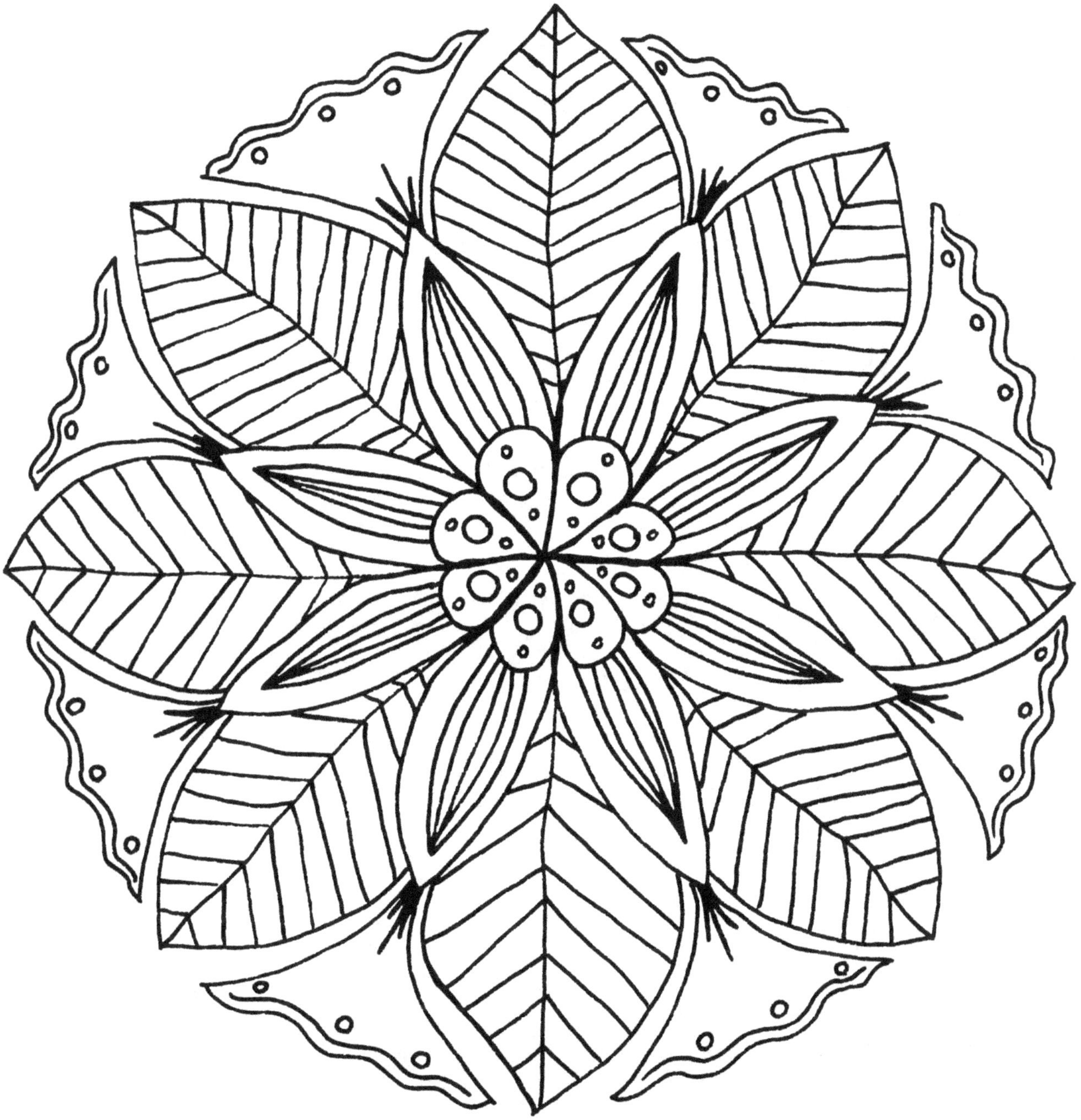

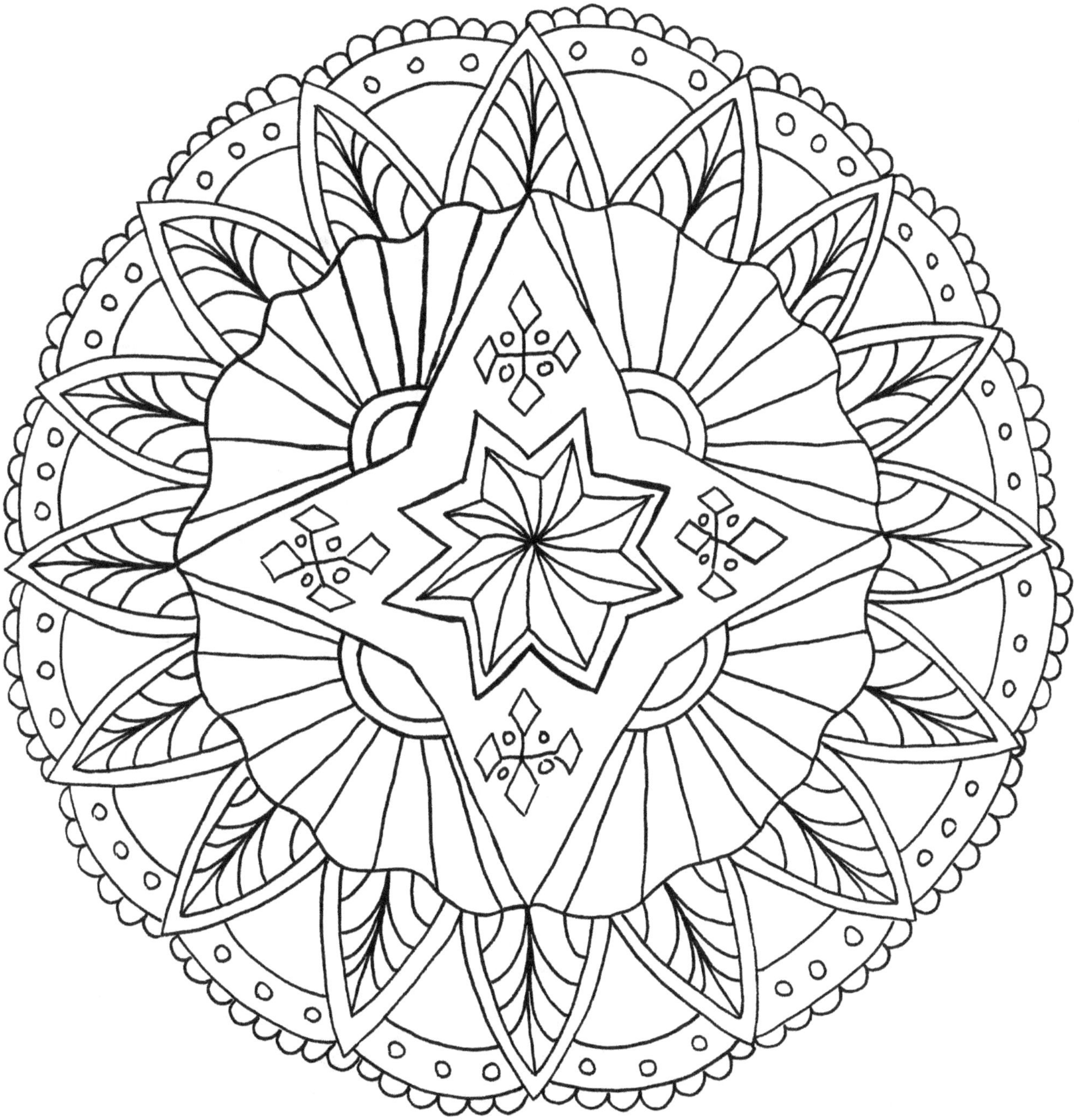

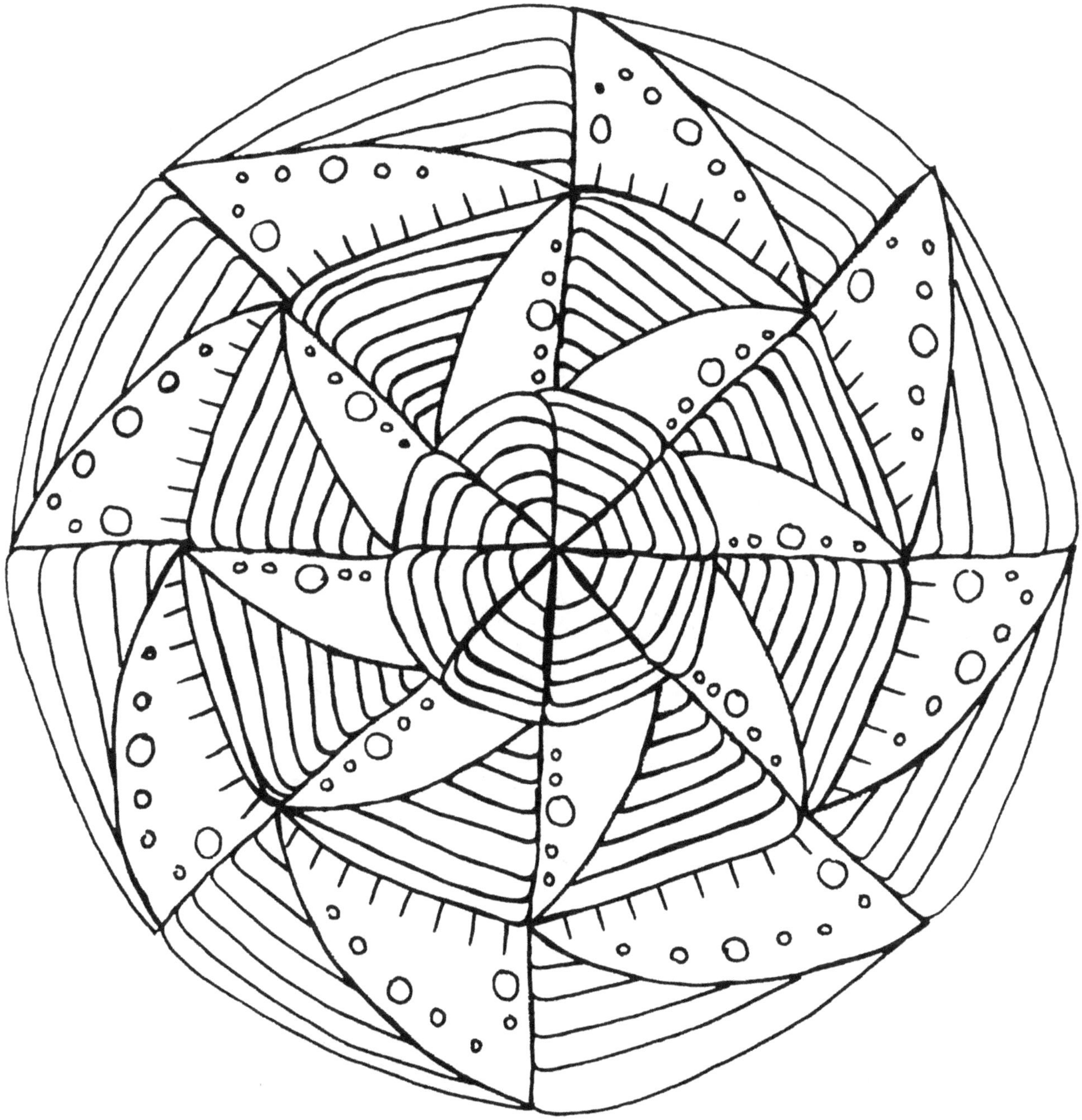

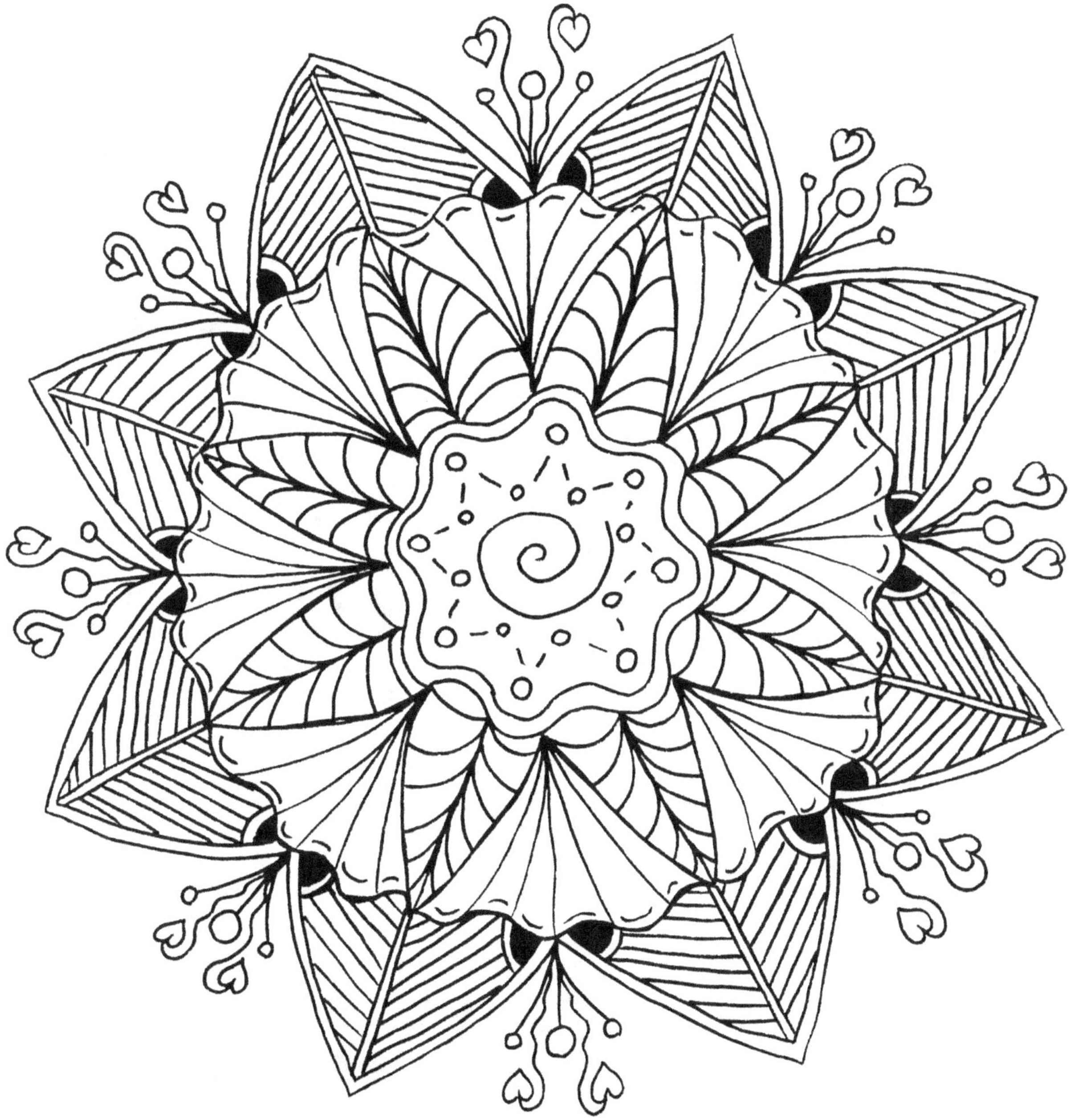

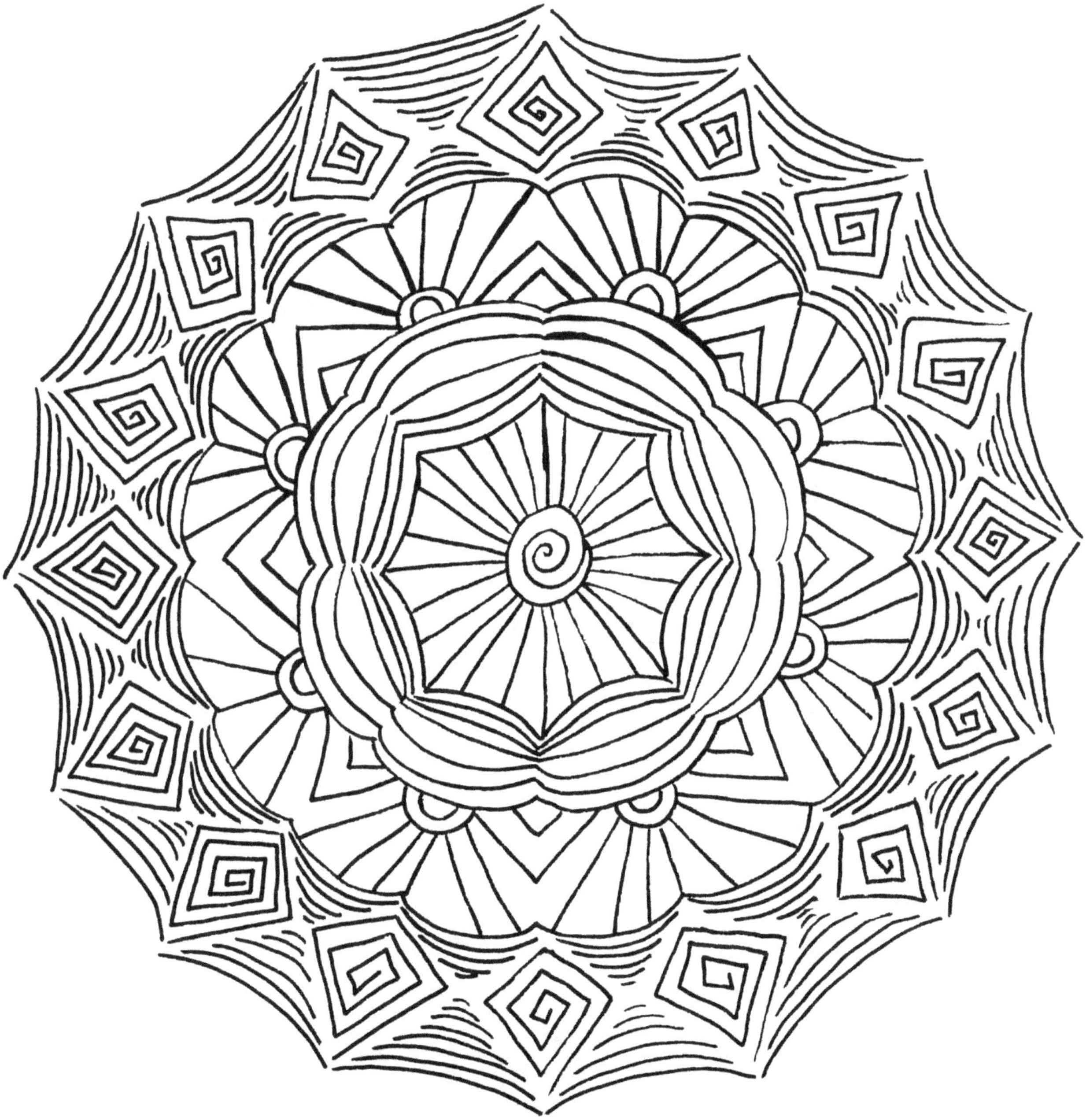

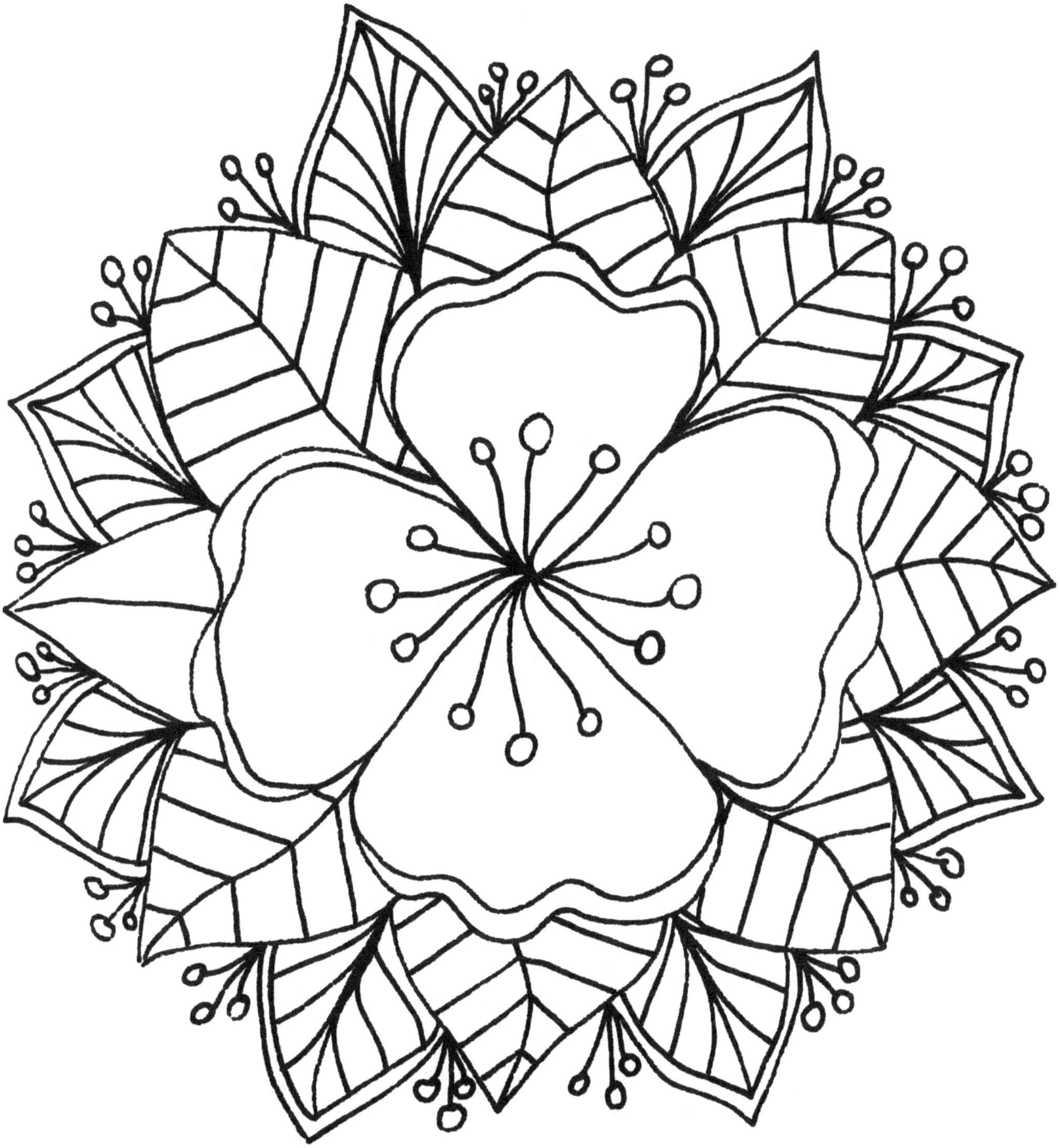

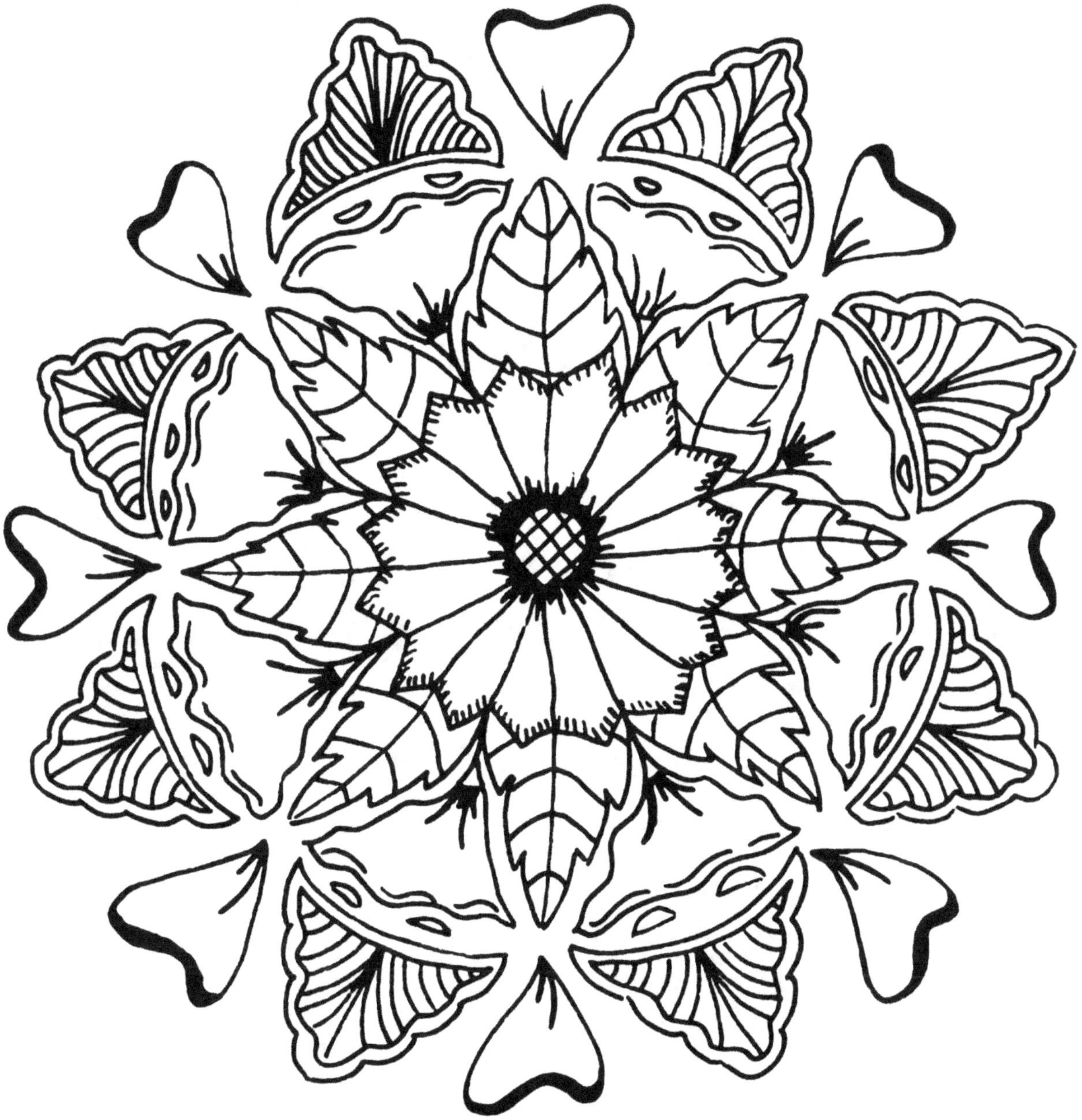

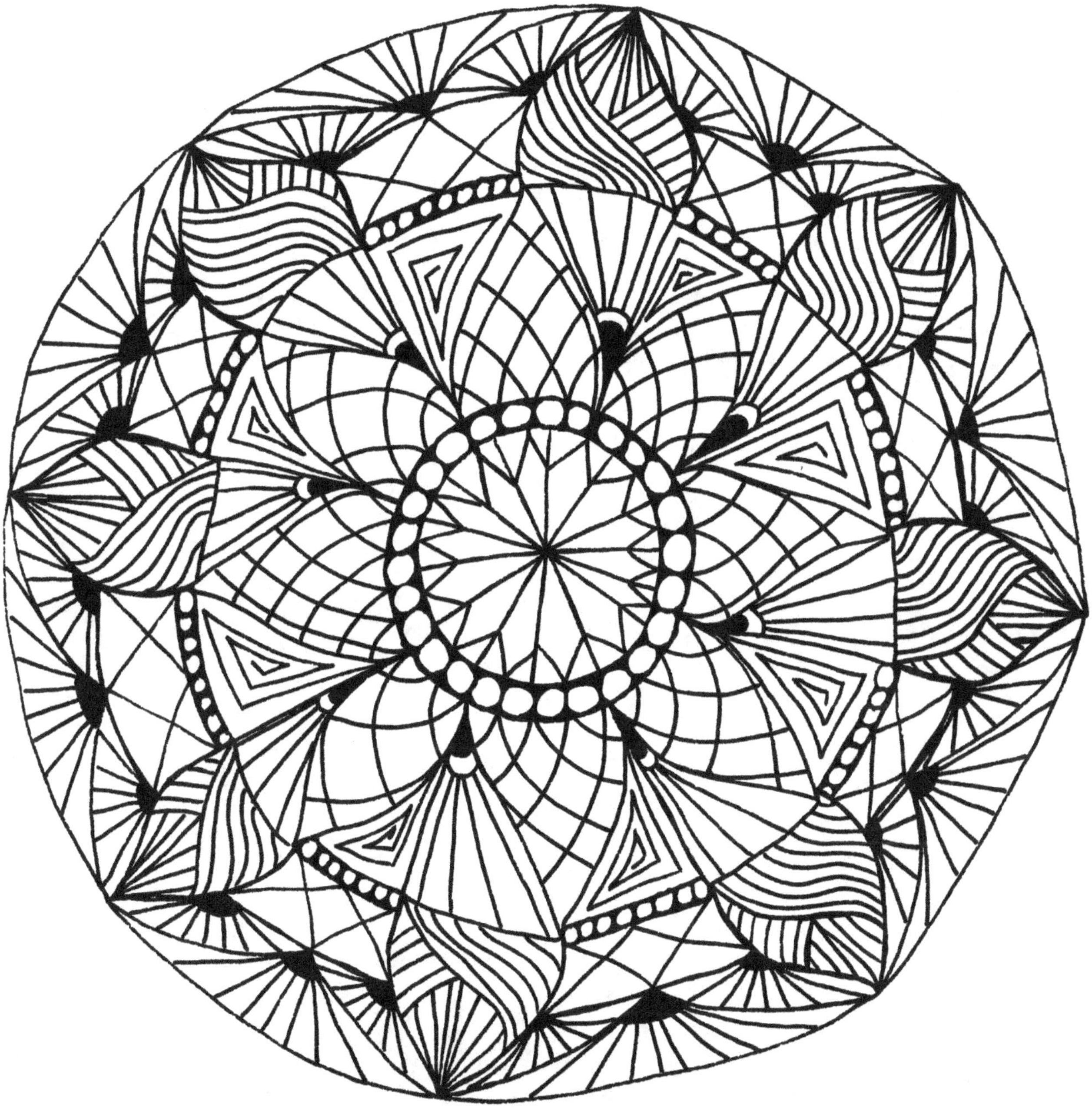

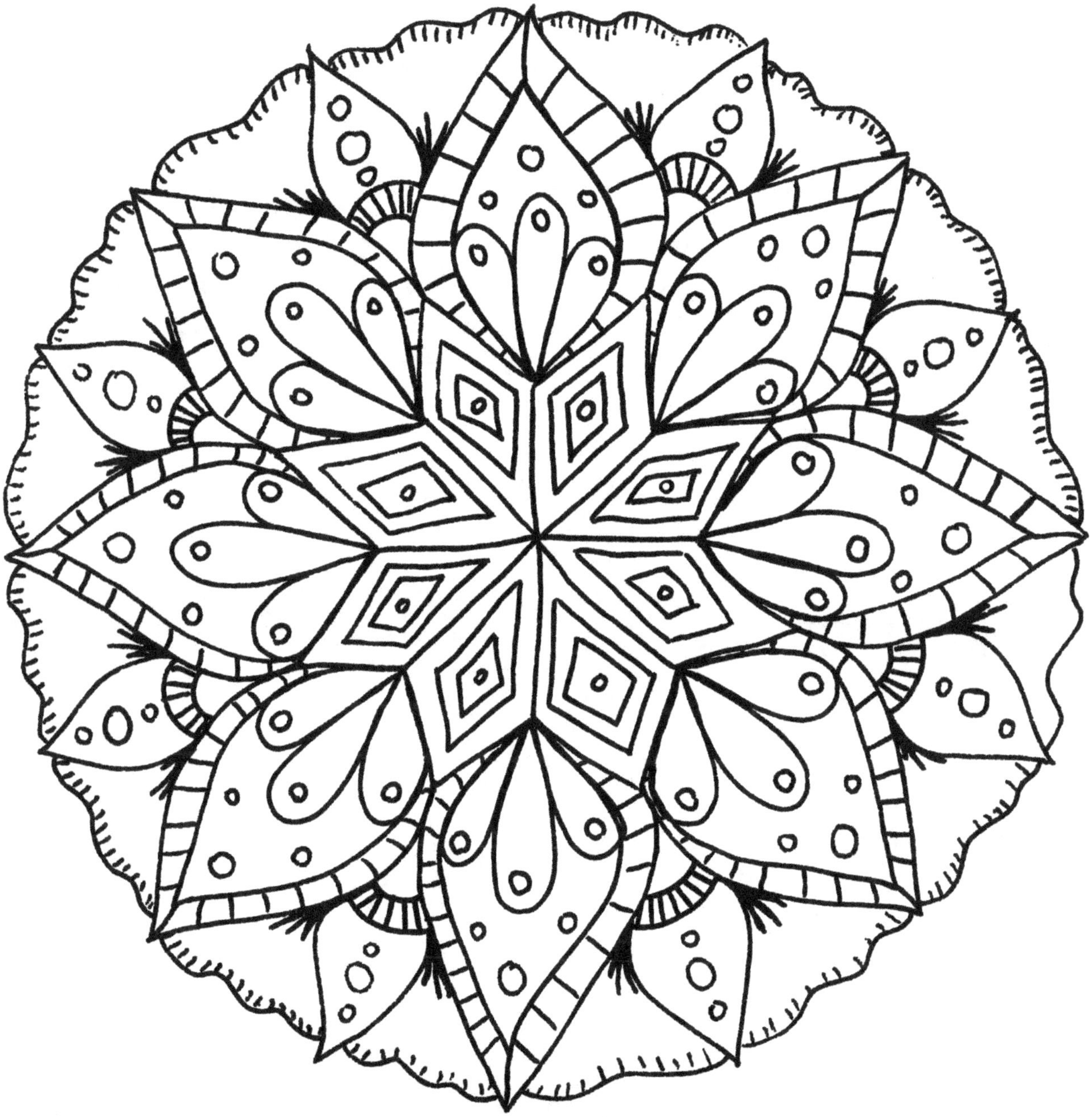

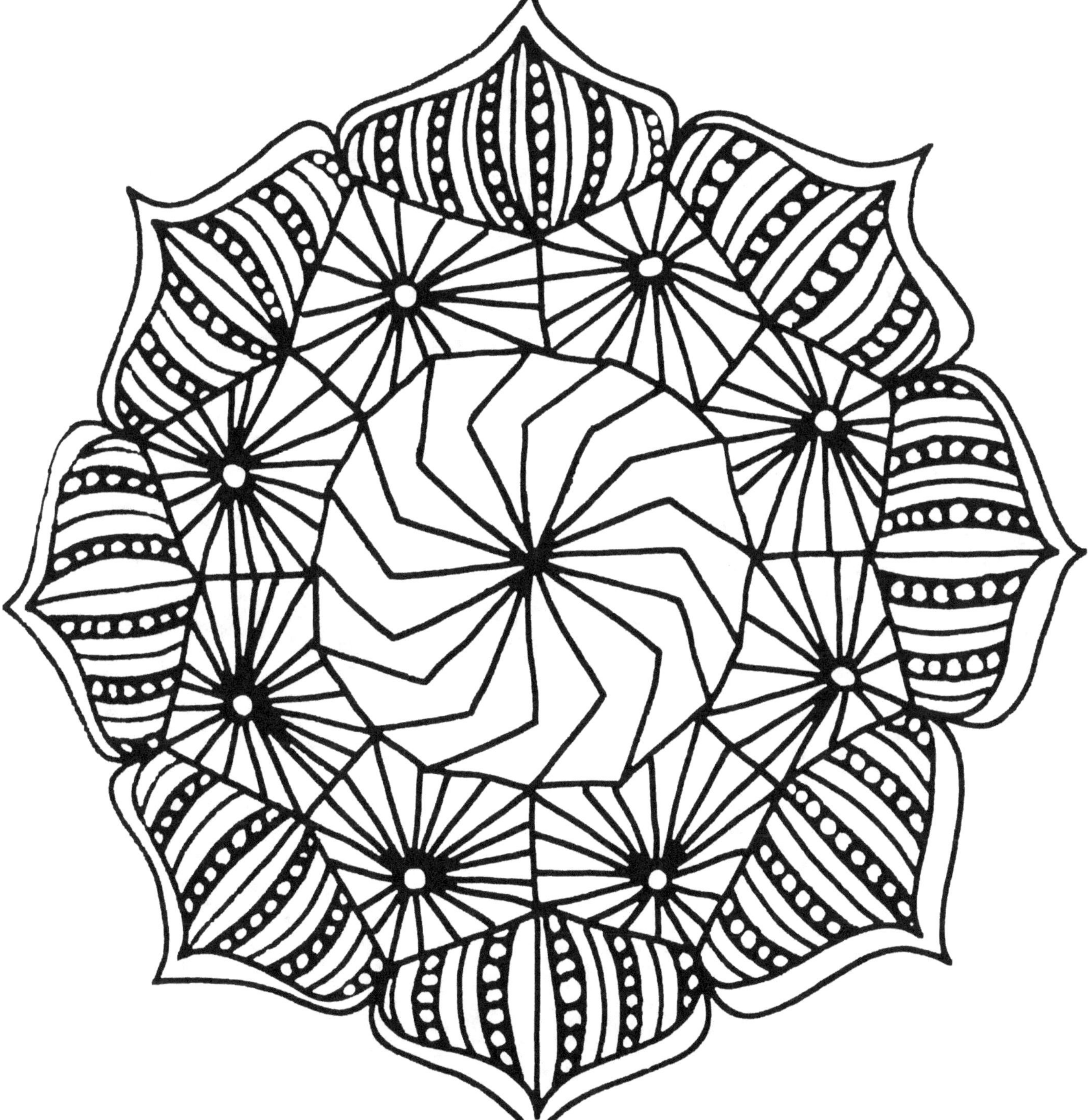

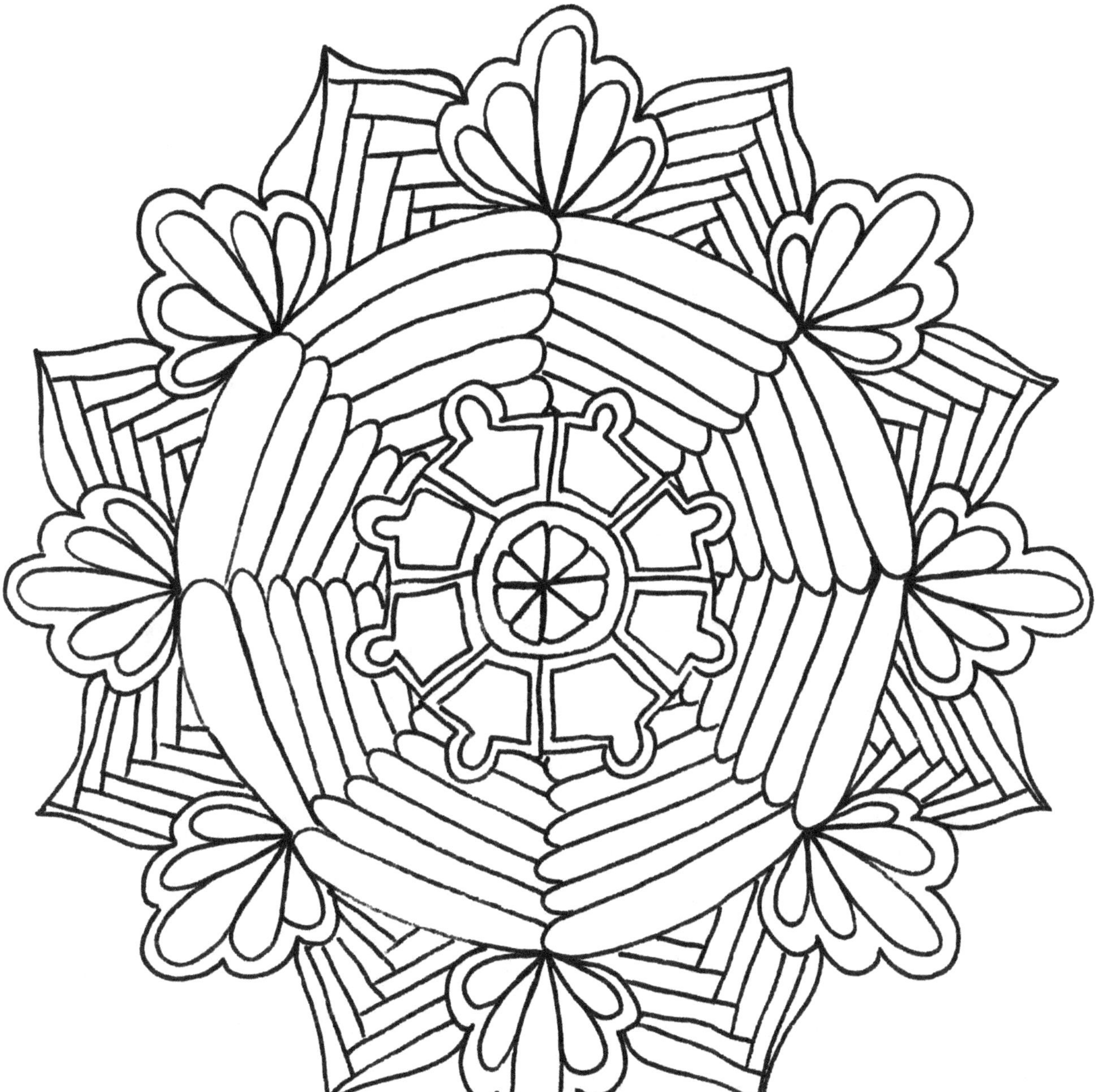

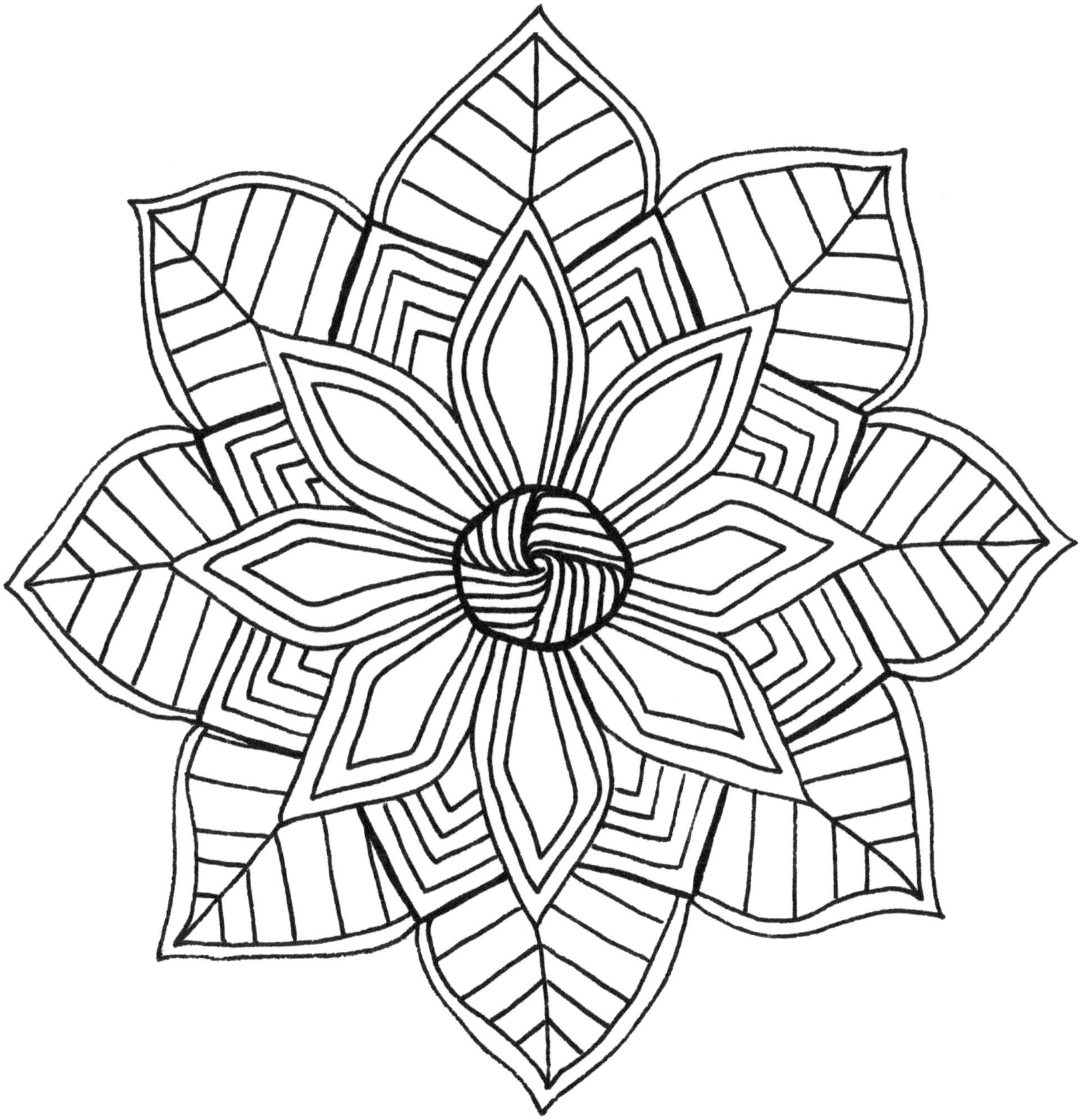

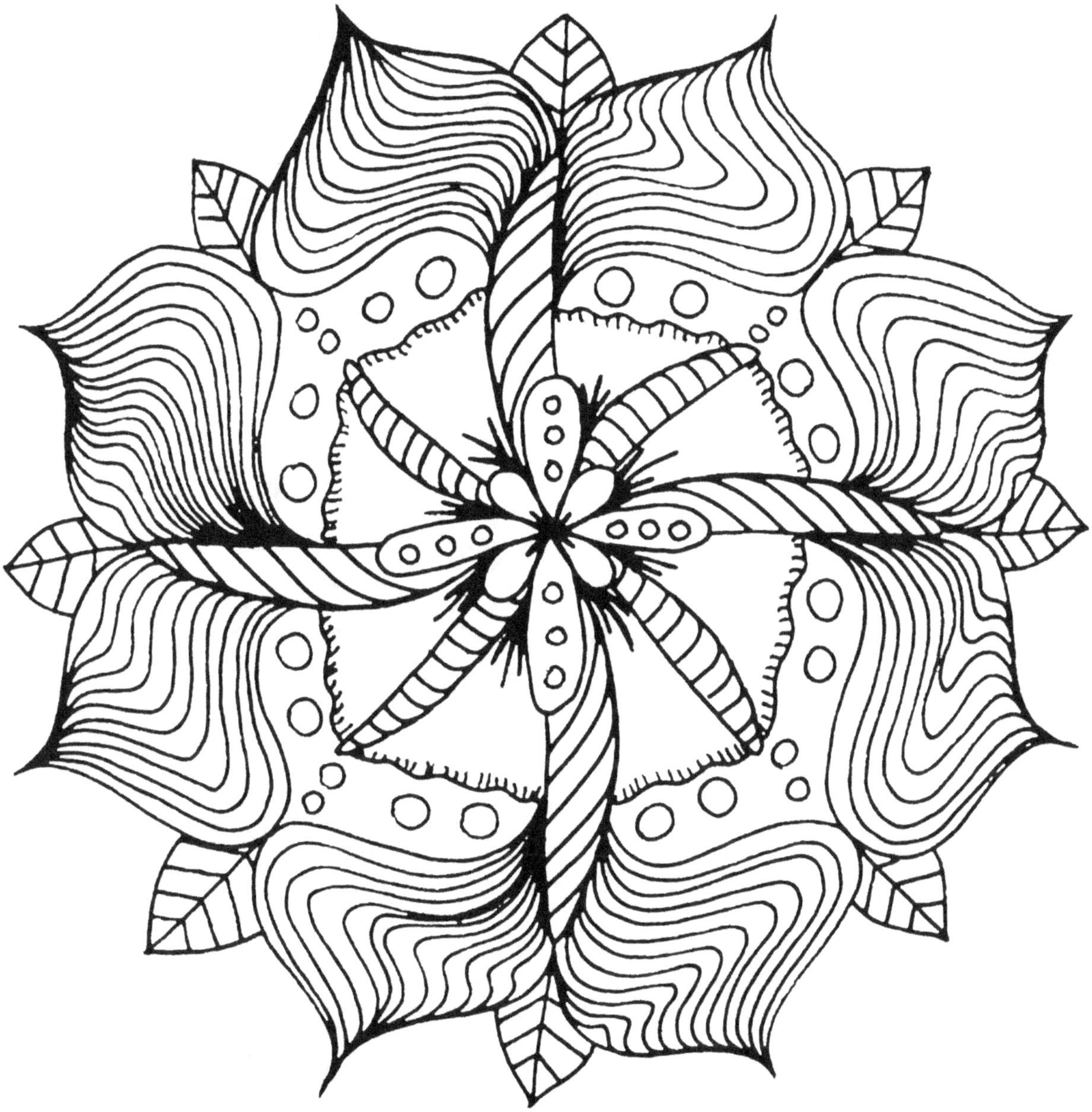

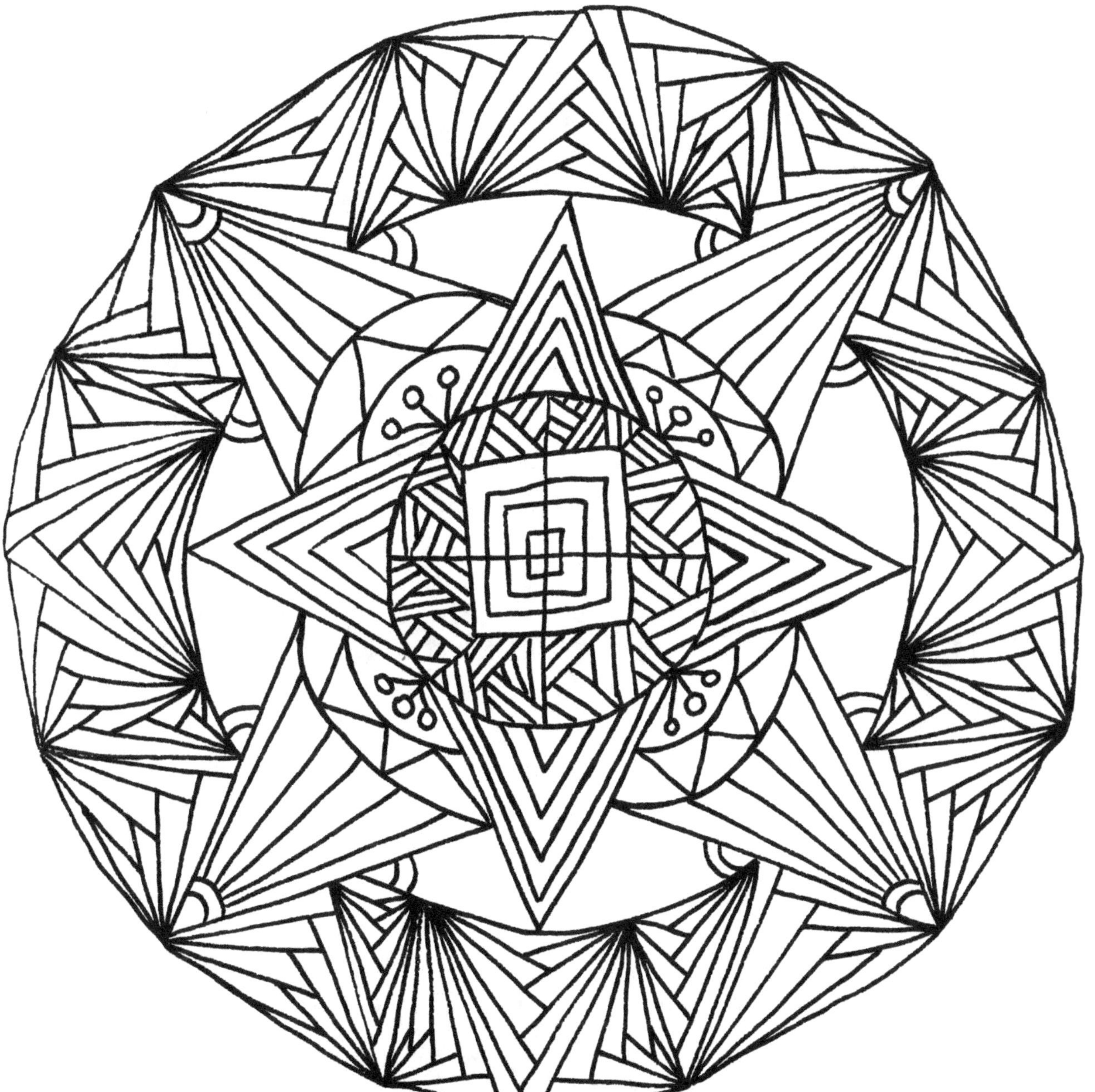

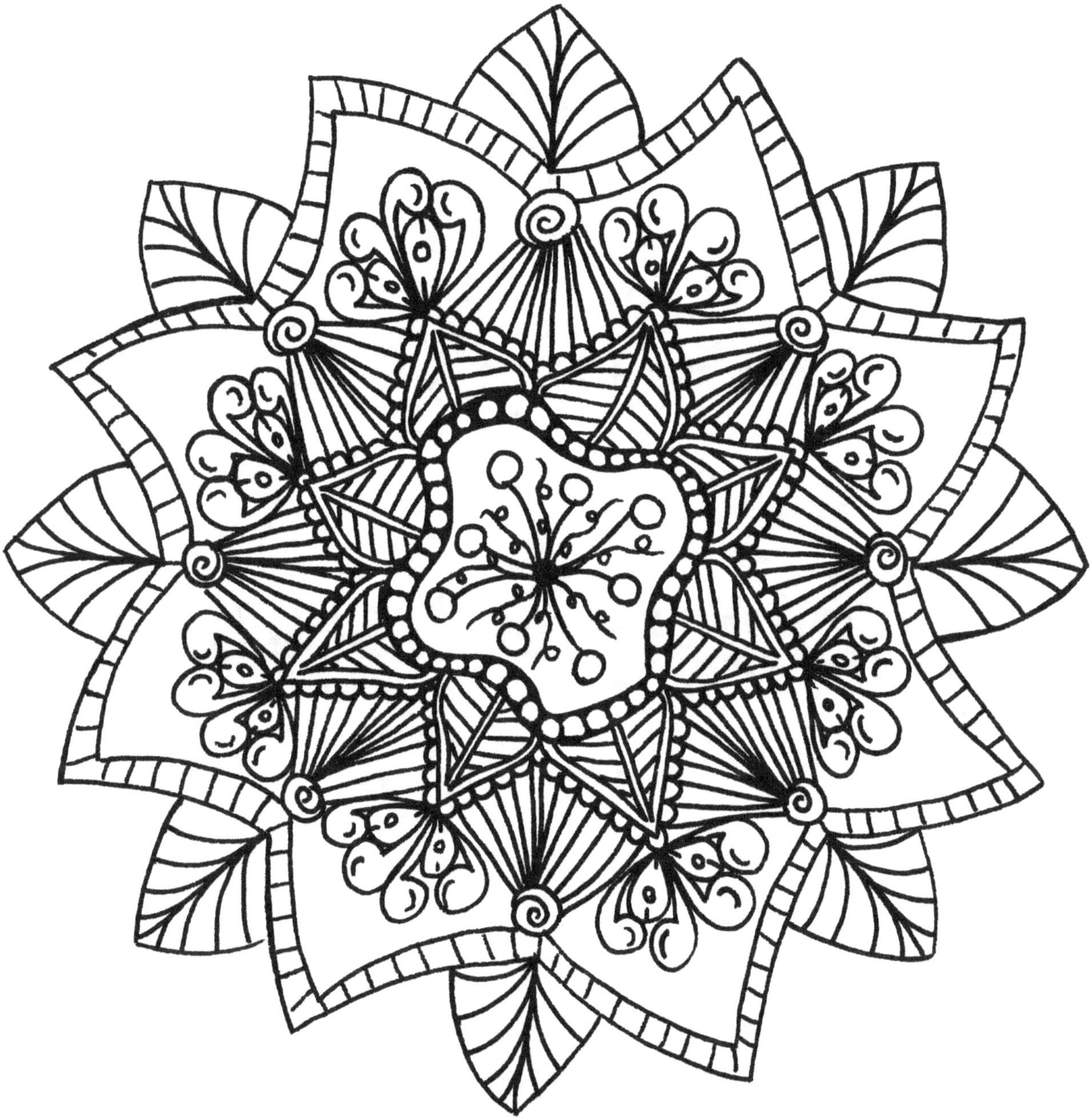

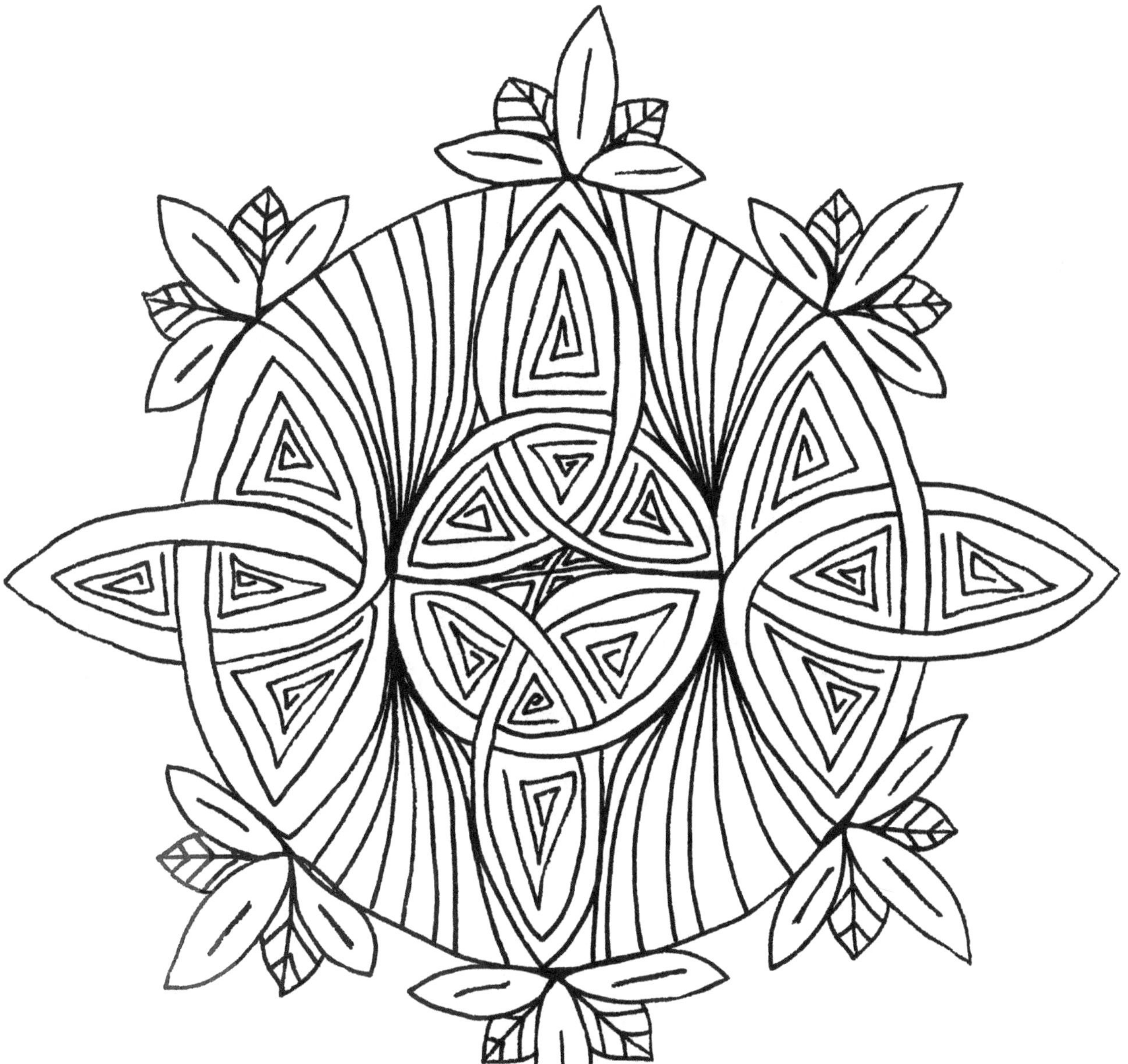

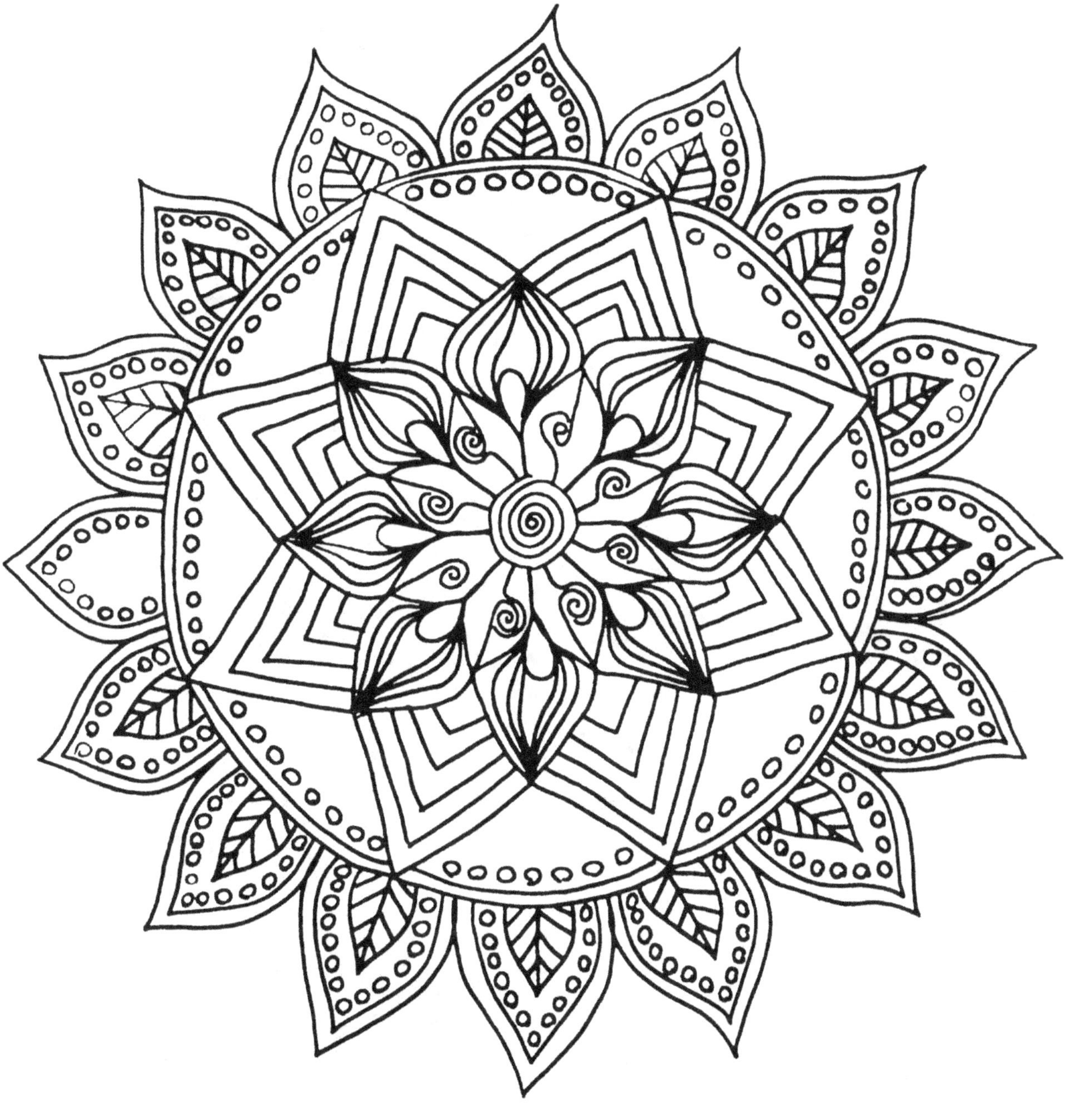

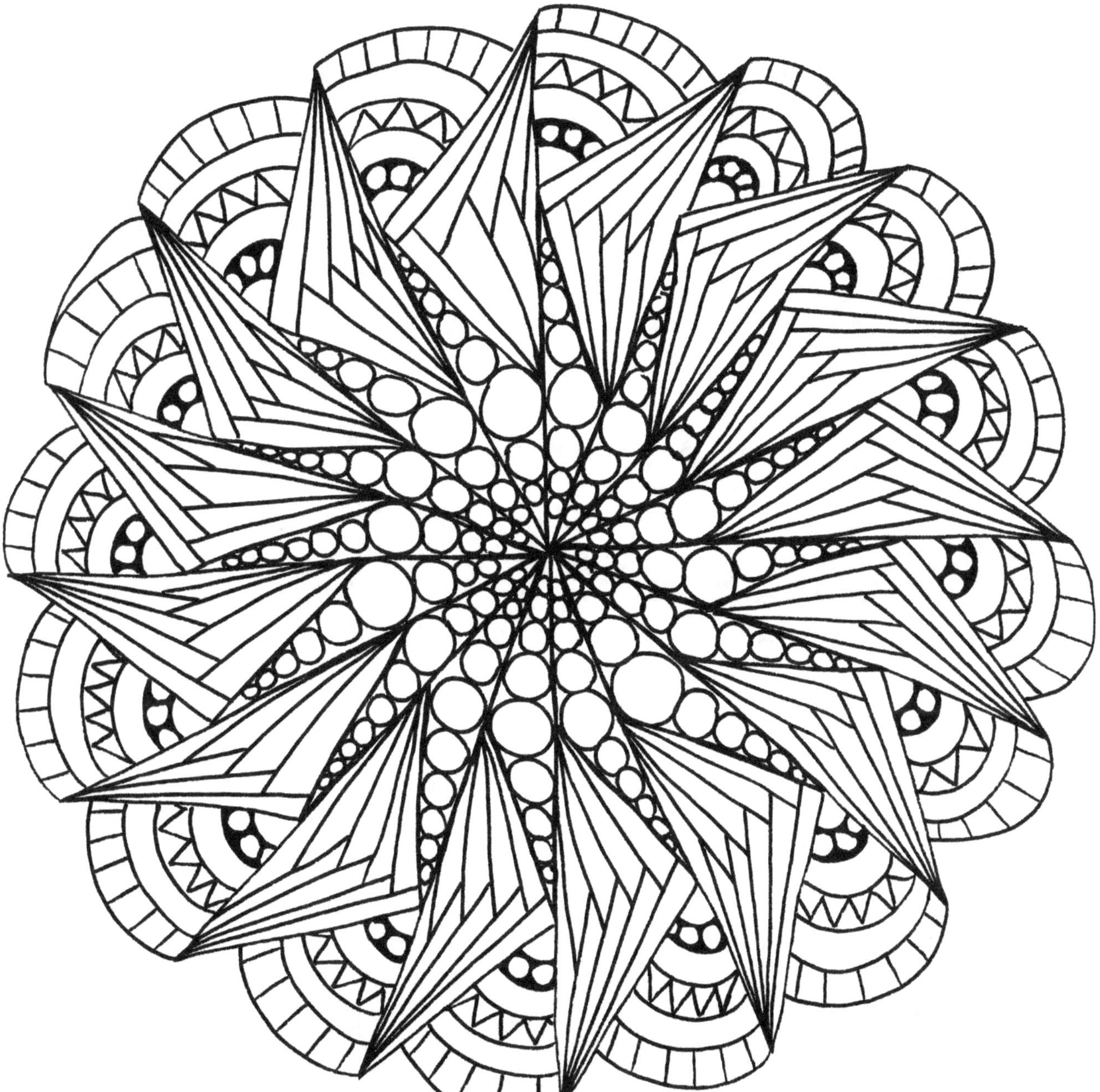

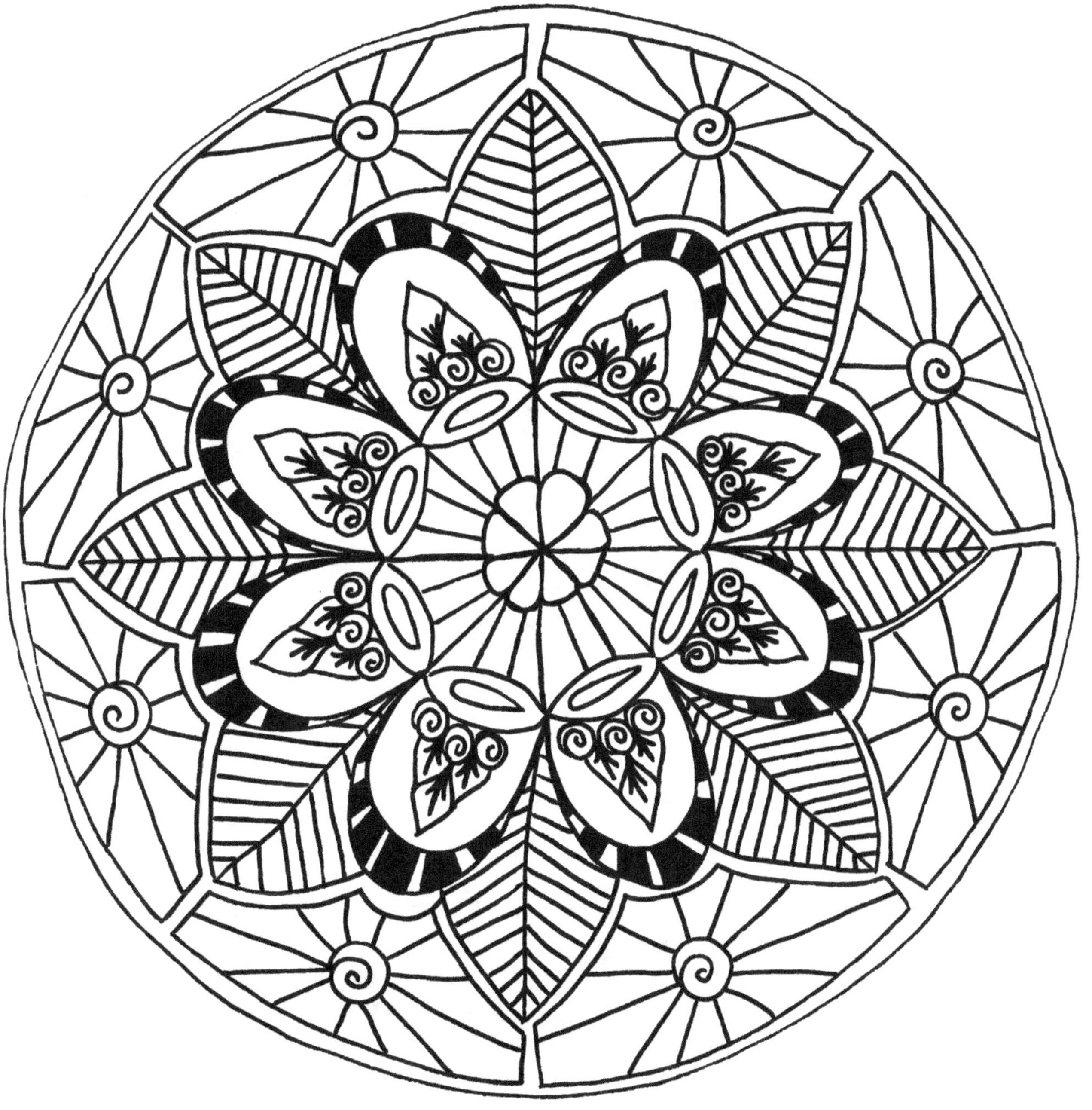

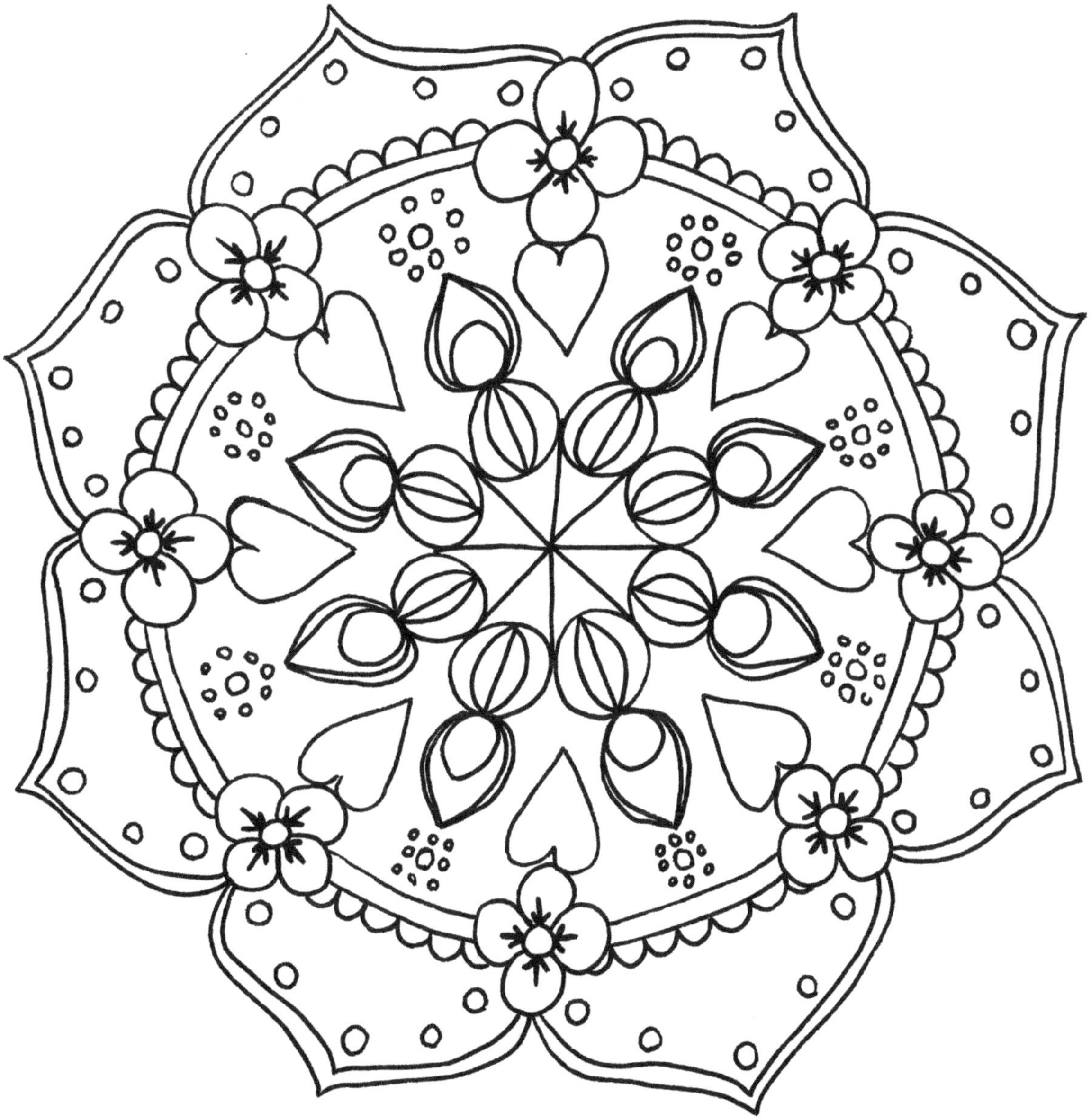

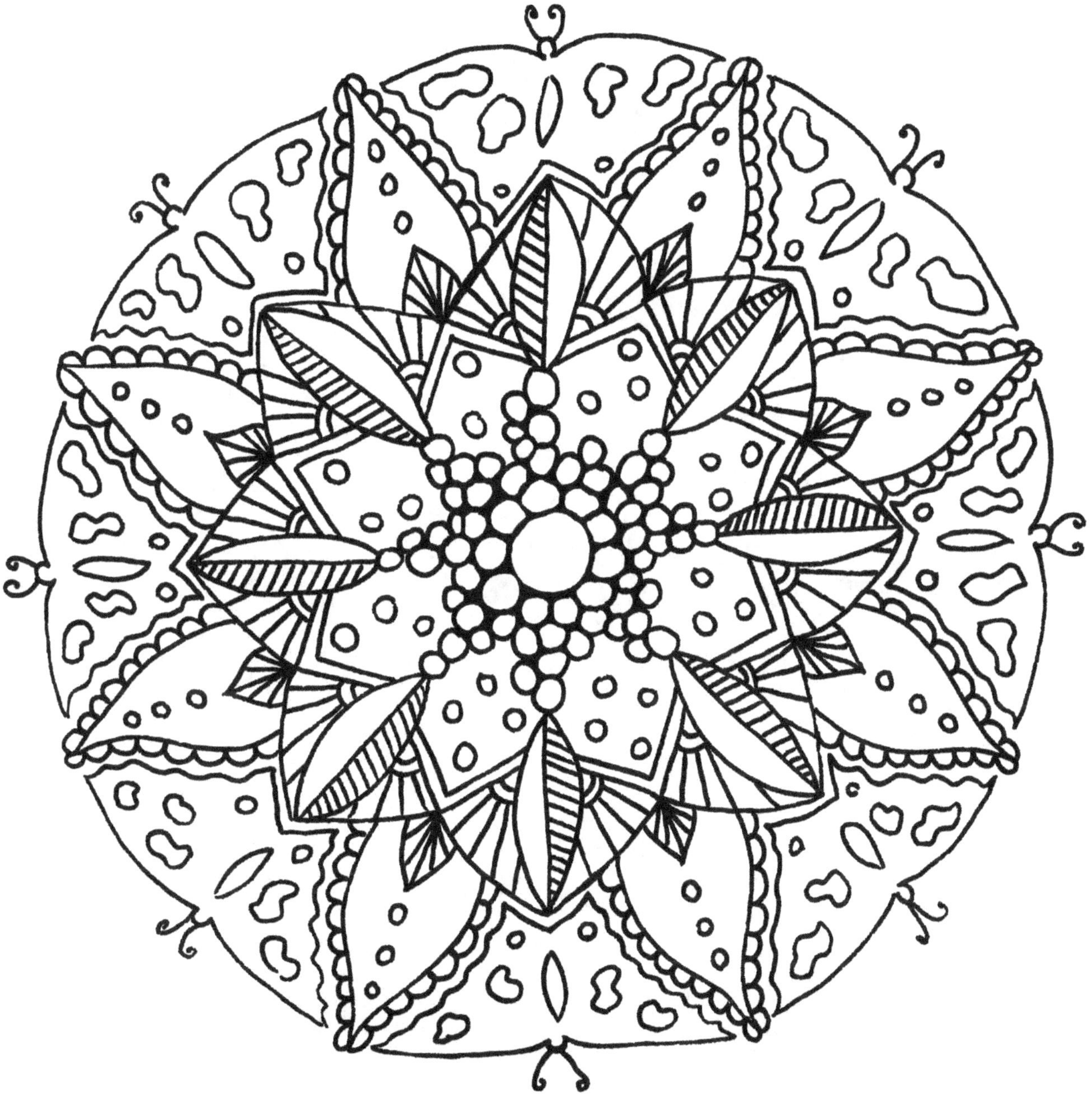

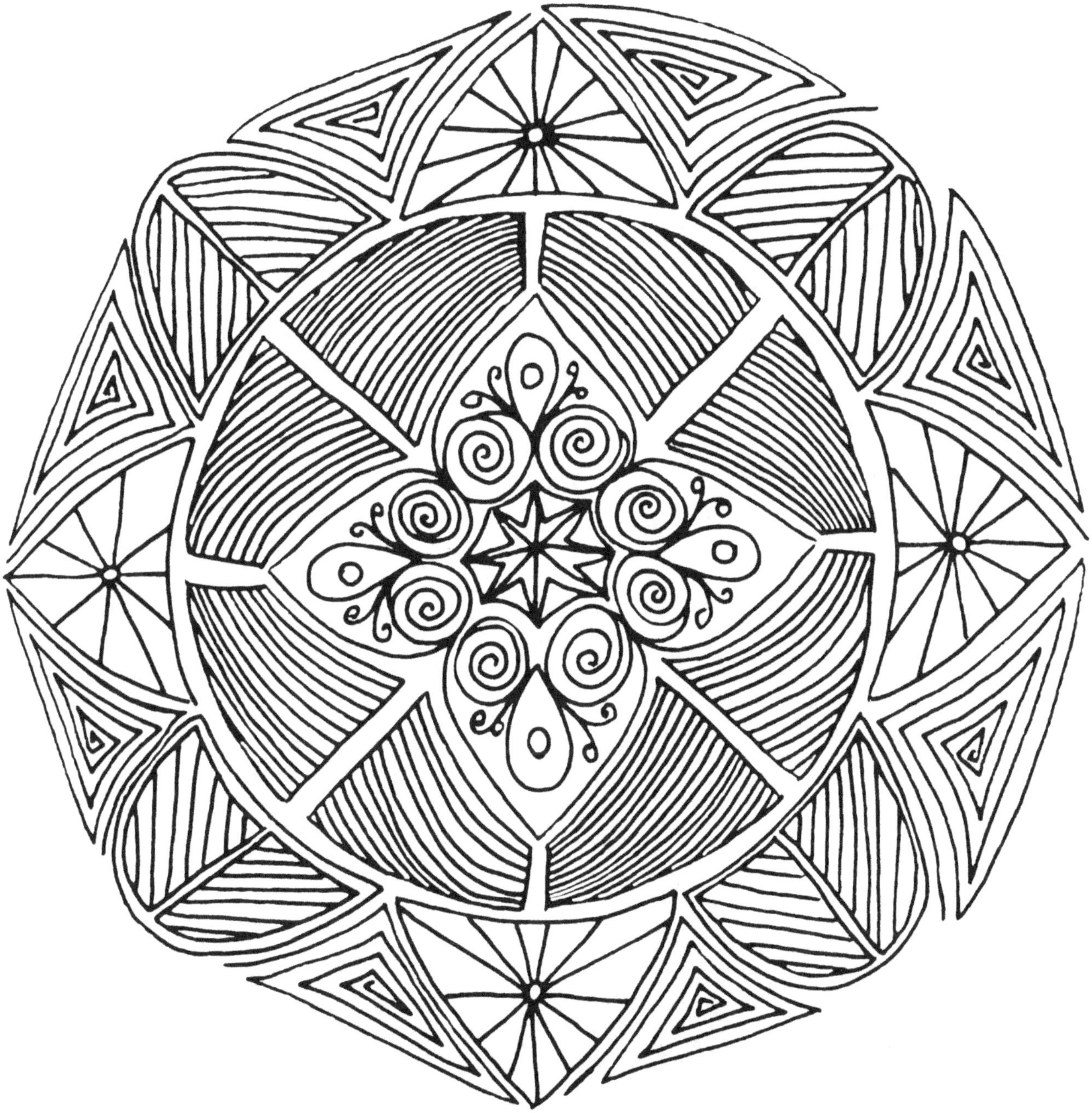

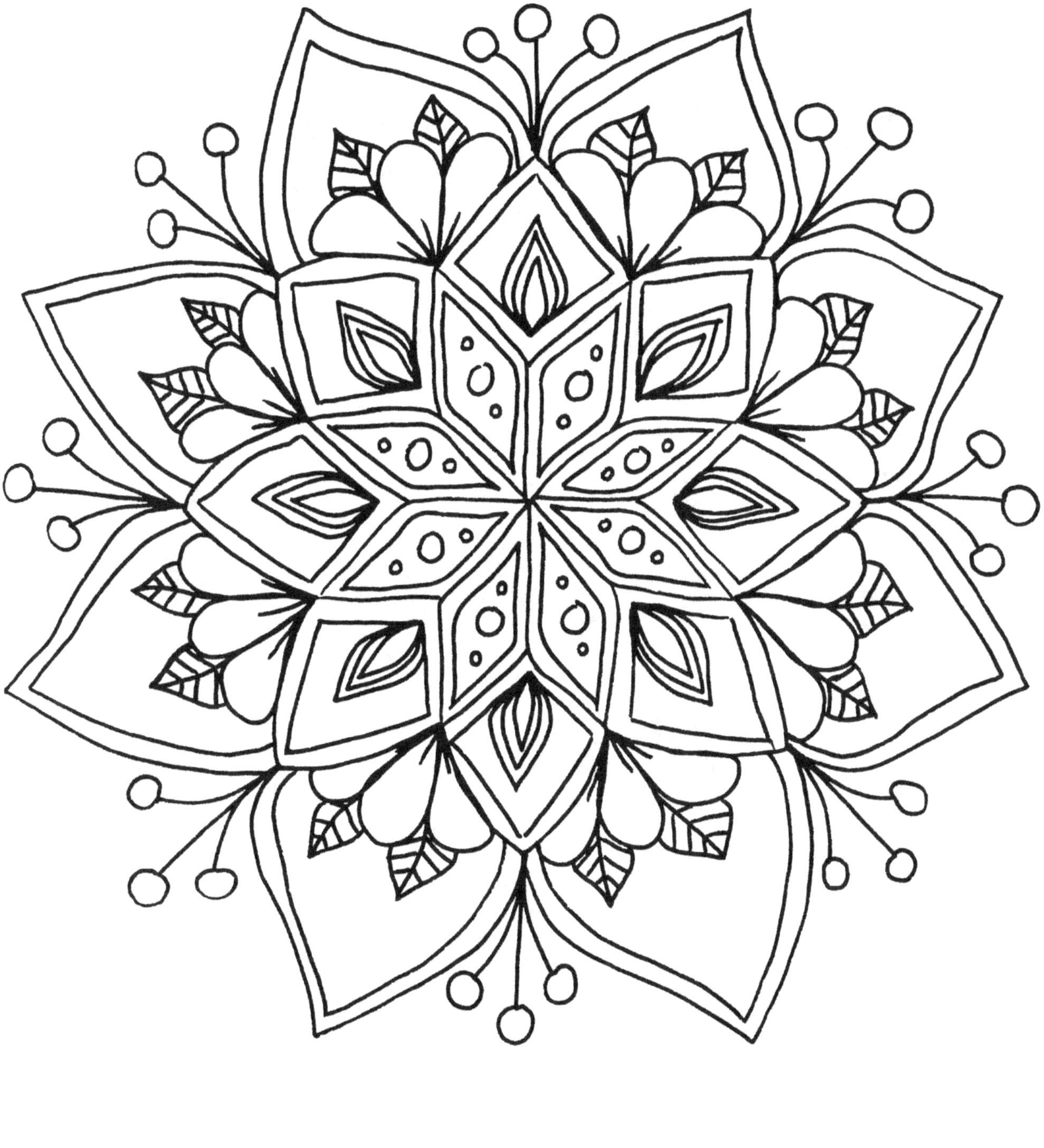

www.ingramcontent.com/pod-product-compliance
Lightning Source LLC
Chambersburg PA
CBHW081255180526
45170CB00007B/2438
* 9 7 8 1 5 4 2 5 6 3 8 1 9 *